Miramichi
Tales tall & true

Best wishes
Doug Underhill

by Doug Underhill
illustrated by Karen Wheaton

Neptune Publishing Company Limited, Saint John, New Brunswick

Miramichi - Tales Tall & True

Miramichi – Tales Tall & True
A paperback original from Neptune Publishing Company Ltd.

The publisher wishes to acknowledge and thank the Department of Municipalities, Culture and Housing for their assistance in this publication.

Canadian Cataloguing in Publication Data
ISBN 1-896270-11-5
Underhill, Doug 1946 -
Folklore, ghost stories and legends of the Miramichi 1. Folklore -- New Brunswick -- Miramichi River Region. 2. Ghost Stories, Canadian (English) -- New Brunswick -- Miramichi River Region. 3. Legends -- New Brunswick -- Miramichi River Region. I. Title.
GR113.5.N48U6 1999 398.2'09715'21 C99-950132-I

Printed in Canada

Cover Design, Typesetting and Layout by Cameron Alexander Designs

Illustrations by Karen Wheaton

Neptune Publishing Company Ltd.,
P.O. Box 6941, Station A
Saint John, New Brunswick E2L 4S4
(506) 847-0376

Table of Contents

Table of Contents

Dedication

This book is dedicated
to Manford Wasson,
John (Jack) Ullock
and the late
Tom Donovan.

Acknowledgements

Writing a book is never an easy job. Although it is only the author's name that finally appears on the cover, a book such as this would not have become a reality without the assistance of a good many people.

Almost every story in this book was the result of people who were willing to share their ideas and stories. Without them my work would not have been possible. There were those who told me stories, others who knew people who knew stories, some who had photos, those who loaned me materials, those who allowed me to use some of their material and those who actually went out and did some research for me. Others helped in the technical end with scanning photos and trouble shooting computer problems. There were even those who helped by encouraging me while I was doing the work and those who were my sounding boards and helped with the first draft. There was Karen Wheaton my illustrator, and Susan Flood of Neptune Publishing who served as professional editor. And of course there was my family who allowed me their time to work on the book.

Special thanks to Manford Wasson who has been my sounding board and a very valuable source of information. I also would like to thank Tom Donovan, Jack Ullock, Rev. B. M. Broderick, Edmond Robichaud, Morris and Peggy Green, Harold Adams, Fred Adair, Rev. Vincent Donovan, Carl Burns, Delphine Harris, Madeline and Mickey Augustine, Edward Estey, Peter Manderson, Patricia Hubbard, Micah Blakely, Stanley MacDonald, Theresa Kelly, Allan Kelly, Eugene Gillis and family, Ralph Thompson, Dean Gillis, Perley Tozer, Frank McKibbon, Peter and Elaine McKibbon, Susan Butler, Wayne Curtis, Bill Allen, Gerry Morris, Clyde Johnson, Ed Russell, Graeme Russell, Stanford McKibbon's family, Rev. Henry McGrath, Terry Whalen Jr., Donnie Ross, George Carney, Joe Breen, Barbara MacIntosh, Margaret Anderson, Frank Waye, Ned Creamer, Jackie Fallon, Eugene Donovan, Farrell McCarthy, Dale MacRae, Jimmy Lawlor, John McKay, the family of Lucky Gray and others.

It is always impossible to name all who have helped directly and indirectly by encouraging me to continue. To all, you realize that this is your book as much as it is mine and I am deeply grateful for your efforts.

Doug Underhill
Miramichi, N.B.

Introduction

The Miramichi is defined by its river and its people. Together they create a mystical union and sense of identity. Wherever the river runs, be it from Baie Ste. Anne to above Boiestown, or Sunny Corner, Sillikers and Red Bank to Wayerton, everyone feels him/herself a Miramichier. The Miramichi is perhaps the most unique area of the province in as much as it has this sense of identity and cohesiveness spread over such a distance. It is part of this feeling that I have tried to capture in this book.

I was born a Miramichier and am very proud of it. The river flows through me shaping my thoughts and feelings. It is a primeval mother for me as it is for all who live on and with it.

The Miramichi has its own unique way of speaking that is rich in metaphor. It is a melting pot of many cultures including Micmac, English, French, Irish and Scottish, and yet these all blend into a character that is distinctly Miramichi.

Geographically, the center of the province is in the Miramichi, and for Miramichiers, it does not matter how far they travel, there is a yearning to come home. Miramichiers are like the salmon that give the river a good part of its character. There is a life long desire to return.

It is out of this love for the people and the region that I have tried to present and preserve a part of our culture. Parts of this book contain familiar people and stories while other parts concentrate on stories and people which have not been given the permanence of print in previous works.

The Miramichi has provided a great portion of the world with fish, lumber and sailing ships during the last century. Stone for the Parliament Buildings of Canada also came from our land.

The Miramichi was home to Premiers Lemuel Tweedie and Frank McKenna, and John James Fraser, Lieutenant-Governors, Lemuel Tweedie, J. R. Snowball and J. Leonard O'Brien, and Senators Percy Burchill, Margaret Anderson and Norbert Theriault. Our forbearers also include two Fathers of Confederation Peter Mitchell and John Mercer Johnson and politicians such as Lord Beaverbrook who served in England's government. In literature we have David Adams Richards, a two time Governor-General's Award winner in fiction and non-fiction. We have sent hockey players Jack Keating, Eddie Wiseman and Greg Malone to the NHL, and Jason Dickson to the Anaheim Angels and the Major League Baseball All Star Game. Women's Hockey Olympic Silver Medalist Kathy McCormack and world class boxer Yvon Durelle are from the Miramichi. We have won national baseball and hockey titles. We are known the world over for our salmon fishing. And we have welcomed the world here.

There are those who have walked the world stage and those who have shone here at home, but they are first and foremost Miramichiers. If in any way, this book has helped in preserving even the smallest part of what it means to be from the Miramichi, I am satisfied.

The Miramichi

When the term Miramichi is used, it is a multi-levelled concept. The Miramichi is a river, a city, a community, a region and a state of mind. It is unique and special in its own way. When local hockey broadcaster Hoppy Dunn began his radio telecasts, it was with "Hello, hockey fans from the head waters of the Miramichi to the farewell buoy."Dunn captures in spirit what the term "Miramichi" means.

Located on the northeast coast of New Brunswick the Miramichi encompasses virtually all of Northumberland county, an area of some 4,720 square miles. Its main artery is the Miramichi River itself which is the second longest river in the province.

In his book *River Guides of the Miramichi* Wayne Curtis writes:

"The Miramichi is one of the great river systems of our land; in fact, it is one of the most famous salmon rivers of the world. In fishing journals and angling brochures, it is described as 'the mother of all salmon rivers'".

The Miramichi River begins in Miramichi Bay some 25 miles across at Escuminac about 30 miles below the former town of Newcastle, and journeys inland making its first branch about three miles above the former town at Beaubear's Island, breaking into the Main Southwest which continues through Renous, Blackville, Doaktown and well above Boiestown to its source near the village of Juniper, a distance of close to 75 miles.

The other branch, The Northwest Miramichi heads up into Red Bank and Sunny Corner where it branches into the Little

Southwest Miramichi and the Northwest which continues close to Heath Steele Mines.

So much a part of the identity of a Miramichier is this river that one could find himself on the North Branch of the Little Southwest Branch of the Northwest Branch of the Main Miramichi and know exactly where he was.

First inhabited by the Micmacs, it is said that the word Miramichi comes from their language, and according to Louise Manny in *Songs of Miramichi* is believed "to be the oldest [Native] place name still in use in North America".

According to Manny no one knows where the derivation of the word comes from. She credits historian Robert Cooney as inventing "a fanciful meaning" which translates as "Happy Retreat".

The historian Dr. W. F. Ganong maintained the name "Miramichi" was given to the area by Montagnais of Gaspe who feared the Micmacs and referred to the area as "The country of the Bad People".

Whatever its source and meaning, Miramichi has that mysterious mystical essence about it that still gives outsiders nightmares in pronunciation as they tend to accent the latter part of the word instead of placing the loudest sound on the first syllable.

Following the Micmacs, the area was visited by a variety of European explorers who gradually brought it into their history. There is speculation the Vikings had visited the area as early as 1,000 A.D. and that Basque fishermen were regular visitors, but the first official documents have Jacques Cartier entering Miramichi Bay in 1534.

Miramichi was later part of a large grant of land given to Nicholas Denys and his son Richard in 1653 by France. It was then part of the retreat of the Acadians who were expelled from Nova Scotia in 1755.

Many Acadians made their way up the Miramichi under the leadership of Boishebert who formed a colony on what is now Beaubear's Island just above the former town of Newcastle. The French

Fort at what is now French Fort Cove was built to protect this colony from English attack.

It is said that General Wolfe, Commander of the English, sent one of his commanders up the Miramichi River in pursuit, burning a colony along the north side of Miramichi Bay which is now known as "Burnt Church".

In the years following, Miramichi rose to prominence in the fishing, lumbering and shipbuilding industries. In 1765 Scotsmen William Davidson, the first English speaking settler on the river, and John Cort arrived in Miramichi and were awarded a 100,000 acre grant of land with the expectation that they were to clear and farm it.

However, the rich fishery including the salmon stocks were more attractive. Settlers claimed that they could not sleep at night due to the constant noise made by salmon jumping. Davidson then opened a shipyard in 1773 and his men built and launched the first ship from the area appropriately christened "Miramichi".

Miramichi became the center of a flourishing lumbering industry. Established as a settlement in 1786, Newcastle, at the turn of the nineteenth century had a population of 1,000 and Chatham, given its name by Francis Peabody, was a lively seaport. Shipbuilding yards were numerous with close to 30 on the river, and the lumbering trade was given a healthy shot in the arm during the Napoleonic Wars when the Baltic ports were closed to Britain.

This placed a huge demand on Miramichi to furnish masts for the King's Navy from the large white pines which were native to the area. Almost every small community had a saw mill and industry was booming. It is reported that at any one time up to 125 vessels could be counted on the river.

Louise Manny records that there approximately 500 ships built in Miramichi at this time.

Miramichi witnessed an influx of immigrants including United Empire Loyalists following the American Revolution, as well as settlers from Scotland and from Ireland, particularly during the potato famine. On the evening of October 6, 1825 tragedy struck. The Great Miramichi Fire nearly wiped out the whole valley, destroying approximately 6,000 square miles. Spreading from near the Nashwaak to below Loggieville in over 10 hours it devastated the area. It created its own hurricane force winds and was said to be the third largest fire ever recorded in history at that time. Only 12 of 260 buildings in Newcastle survived.

Miramichiers would not be discouraged. They rebuilt quickly. Shipbuilding continued to thrive, hitting its high point around 1850. Lumbering and fishing were booming. Jabez Bunting Snowball employed over 900 men at his mill. Other great entrepreneurs such as Joseph and Henry Cunard, Gilmore and Rankin, R. R. Call and John C. Miller, W. S. Loggie, A. & R Loggie, Peter Mitchell, Edward Sinclair, C. C. Watt, D. & J. Ritchie Co., Hutchison and T. W. Crocker continued to help make Miramichi grow and prosper.

The creation of the Intercolonial Railway around 1870 due to the efforts of Peter Mitchell greatly helped the area, particularly as the advent of the steamship began to put an end to the glory days of wooden ships on the Miramichi.

Lumbering remained the prominent industry with families like the Ritchies and the Burchills taking the forefront by the turn of the century. With World War I, there was a great need for pitprops which were temporary wooden uprights used to support the roofs in the coal mine. The Miramichi Mills worked hard to supply some of them.

During the 1920's W. S. Anderson Co. produced large quantities of spoolwood made from white birch. The company had several mills which made products such as basket bottoms, the wood for crates for Singer Sewing Machines, and spoolwood which was shipped to the U.S. and Scotland to be used for making handles and especially spools for thread. The old "square piles" close to where the Miramichi Civic Centre is today was a familiar sight where the bars of wooden birch were tied in bundles and stacked sometimes eight to twelve feet high.

Tying the bundles provided many a job for young Miramichiers during the summer months. This industry thrived until replaced by plastic in the 1960's. A branch of the Anderson family still operates a mill in Miramichi today.

Chatham was given a big boost with the building of CFB Chatham which housed fighter jets including the famed "Golden Hawks". Nuclear weapons were even stored here during the Cold War, and CFB St. Margaret's was a radar base that was part of the southern radar system.

Heath Steele Mines opened in the mid 1950's giving a stronger economic base to the region, particularly Newcastle.

Fraser's Pulp Mill was built in the late 1940's and has passed through a number of companies. Today it exists as Repap and is in the top three largest coated paper mills in the world.

1995 saw the amalgamation of many of the core communities such as Newcastle, Chatham, Nelson-Miramichi, Douglastown and Loggieville into the City of Miramichi.

Today the Miramichi continues to be unique. It is on the cutting edge of technology with New Brunswick Community College-Miramichi Campus. It still has lumbering and forestry as its leading industry and is still world renowned for the lore of its salmon.

The Miramichi boasts the longest running folk festival in North America with the Miramichi Folksong Festival which will enter its forty-second year in August 1999, and the Miramichi is home of the annual Irish Festival which has become an international draw attracting close to 30,000 visitors each July. The American Bus Association has included The Irish Festival in the top 100 events in North America.

The Miramichi has produced its share of famous sons and daughters. We have had Canada's first Minister of Marine and Fisheries, two Fathers of Confederation, Lieutenant-Governors of the province and premiers.

Our native son Max Aitken now known as Lord Beaverbrook, moved to England and made his fortune publishing newspapers.

Beaverbrook served as Minister of Air Craft Production for Churchill during WW II, and his love of Miramichi folksongs such as "The Jones Boys" eased the tension among world leaders such as Stalin when he sang to them at conferences following the war.

Today David Adams Richards brings fame to our region. He has twice been the recipient of Canada's top literary award, winning the Governor-General's award for both fiction and non-fiction.

The Miramichi has the Augustine Mound, a sacred native burial ground which has produced artifacts dating back to B. C. times and linking the Miramichi with trade routes from Ohio.

We have Light Heavyweight Champion of the British Empire and world class boxer Yvonne Durelle who on a questionable count came within a whisker of dethroning Archie Moore for the world title.

One of the discoverers of insulin, Dr. Banting was married to Henrietta Ball of Newcastle, and Bing Crosby's grandparents on his mother's side (Harrigans) were from the Miramichi. Baseball great Ted Williams became part of the salmon lore of the river. Prime Minister R. B. Bennett studied law here and Prime Minister Brian Mulroney went to college at the former St. Thomas College in Chatham.

Father Ben Murdock wrote "The Red Vineyard". It was one of the more famous books to come out of the first world war. Monsignor Hickey's "The Scarlet Dawn" received the same status in the Second World War.

For a small community, Miramichi has left its mark on the world, and will continue to do so. As local historian Manford Wasson has so aptly stated:

"The Miramichi is a microcosm of the country. We encompass most of the founding ethnic groups of Canada. We have a strong tradition and cultural base from the Native community, the French, the English, the Scottish and the Irish."

Miramichi has had its boom times and times of hardship, but it has always managed to rise above adversity, and continue to grow. Its best resource has always been its people and the spirit they have shown.

Perhaps it is this optimism and sense of enthusiasm which shows naturally when any Miramichier greets another. The conversation will go something like this:

"How she goin' ?"

The answer is always "The very best".

Headless Nun crossing the Crow Brook in French Fort Cove.

Ghost Stories

The Headless Nun

She won't hurt you
She's just alone
She's just asking
Make my body whole.

If you are walking Miramichi's French Fort Cove, be careful, you may not be alone. You could encounter "The Headless Nun" or any of the other spirits which are reported to haunt there.

The Headless Nun is one of the Miramichi's better known ghost stories and a central part of the legend surrounding the French Fort Cove. The story dates back to the mid 1700's when a young nun's knowledge of buried treasure led to her tragic death.

After the Expulsion of the Acadians from Nova Scotia in 1756, many Acadians made their way north towards the French colony of Quebec. Some 3,500 stopped in northern New Brunswick and set up a small community on Beaubear's Island just above the former town of Newcastle.

It was with this community that "The Headless Nun" is thought to have been associated. Historian Harold W.J. Adams who researched "The Tale of the Headless Nun" for the *Miramichi Leader* place mat project gives an historical scenario for "The Headless Nun". He gives her the name "Sister Marie Inconnus" with "Inconnus" being

Latin for "Unknown" and "Marie" a very common religious name frequently used by young women who entered religious orders.

Adams surmises that Marie Inconnus, "was born into a noble family near Beuzeville-la-Guerard, France," where the custom of the times was that, "the youngest daughter was asked to become a religieuse," and was trained, "as a teacher and nurse".

Perhaps Sister Marie Inconnus, "heard stories from her neighbors la famille des Champs de Boishebert about the sufferings of Acadians in the new world and their need for schools and medical facilities... and begged to be allowed to be assigned as a missionary sister in Acadia".

She obtained passage to Quebec in 1750 and eventually made her way to New Brunswick. After the fall of Fort Beausejour in 1755, Charles des Champ De Boishebert gathered the refugee French Acadians and set up a community at Cocagne. It was here he met Sister Marie Inconnus who moved with him when he set up another community known as "Camp d'Esperance" on Beaubear's Island (Boishebert's Island) in July 1756.

In 1758 an English expedition was sent to destroy this community. To protect it, a fort with eight cannons and a variety of muskets was erected at what is now known as French Fort Cove. The Cove is located just below what was then the Town of Newcastle. It was picturesque with rugged terrain. Flowing through it is Crow Brook (Ruisseau a Corneille).

The fort was constructed on the western side of the Cove giving it a formidable view both up and down river. In the event of attack, the fort's cannons had an excellent shooting range in either direction. The fort existed until the late 1700's.

Besides the problem of the British, the Acadians were also besieged by the dreaded disease of leprosy.

Boishebert tried to contain the disease by ensuring that anyone infected not leave the island, but Adams says several of the sailors raging with madness, fled into the darkness of the woods refusing to be imprisoned on the island.

Many of the widows and orphans fearing the approach of the British and wishing to secure a brighter future for themselves and their loved ones, privately gathered all of their valuables, and placed them in an old metal chest.

As the treasures were collected, the value and contents of each family was carefully recorded before the chest was buried. Sister Marie and two other widows were entrusted to find a burial spot to hide the treasure until the danger of a British attack had passed.

In the dead of night under a full moon, Sister Marie and the widows took the chest to French Fort Cove and buried it. Soon after the widows died from scurvy, leaving only Sister Marie with the knowledge of where the chest was buried.

Legend has it that she was returning to the fort one day from delivering a native baby or from her routine duties when a mad trapper lunged out from the woods, grabbed her as she crossed the bridge over Crow Brook. It is said that he cut off her head and then ran off into the forest with it.

Another version of the story has her being attacked by two of the mad sailors who had escaped the island, hoping the buried treasures would buy them safe passage from the area.

It is said the two brutally beat her, but Sister Marie would not divulge the whereabouts of the buried chest. In frustration one sailor grabbed his sword and partially cut off her head. The other, in shock, screamed that he should finish the job. When her head was finally severed, the mad men picked it up , but seeing the horror of her suffering threw the head into the waters of the cove and ran off into the woods.

When the body was discovered the next morning by soldiers going to duty at the fort, there was no head, and an extensive search failed to find it.

Subsequently Sister Marie's body was taken back to Beaubear's Island to be readied for burial. Eventually it was returned to her family in France where it was placed in a crypt at the local cathedral.

However, Sister Marie's spirit has never been at peace. She still looks for her head, and even an ocean has not stopped her search. Her spirit has been sighted numerous times especially during full moons, lurking in French Fort Cove on the bridge over Crow Brook, looking for her head, and more precisely, appearing to various people to ask if they will help her find it.

One story tells of the ghost's offer of 1000 guineas in exchange for her lost head.

Following the demise of the French colony, some time after 1784, the Cove was granted to an Englishman, John Henderson. He used the area as a shipbuilding centre as the Miramichi River's channel was very deep near shore and provided a good place to launch ships.

After the 1860's the Cove was used as the sight of a number of grist mills, which lasted until the turn of the century. Remains of the dam and head pond can still be seen.

On October 6, 1897 there was a flurry of activity when gold was found at the Cove. The excitement resulted from deposits which came up in the borings for a new house being built for the owner of the Dominion Pulp Company Mill. However, nothing further developed.

Then in the 1920's the Buckley Brothers built a huge steam mill and burner at the Cove. The huge brick stack on the down river side of Crow Brook is all that remains of the mill today. It is one of the Cove's most prominent existing landmarks.

The Cove itself has a very rough terrain with its back portions resembling a canyon. These upper portions of the Cove were then used as a quarry producing building stone for the West Block of the Parliament Buildings in Ottawa and for the Cathedral in Charlottetown as well as for local buildings such as the Newcastle Court House, the St. Michael's Basilica in Chatham and Harkins Elementary in Newcastle.

If one walks to the upper end of French Fort Cove it is still possible to see the remains of the old quarry and some of the cut stones still there.

Although much of the physical French influence has vanished, there remain numerous tales of hidden treasures, particularly the secret of the hidden widows' chest which Sister Marie Inconnus took to the grave with her. Even today people feel a strong spiritual presence there.

Many a local treasure hunter has been drawn to the area to search for buried gold and other valuables.

One man told of how he dug for buried treasure by the light of the moon at midnight. Suddenly, his spade struck what appeared to be a buried chest. At this point something white "whooshed" by him, sending him fleeing in terror.

When he returned the next day, he could not find any trace of his spade nor any evidence of where he had dug.

Over the years there also have been stories of French ghosts firing noiseless cannons to scare away the English or anyone who might be seeking their buried treasures.

Former Newcastle mayor and MLA for Miramichi John McKay has several other stories relating to these events.

McKay tells the story of a hotel keeper in Newcastle who didn't believe in banks. As a result he buried his money at French Fort Cove in a keg in the soft soil which is almost like quick sand in some places. As years went on, he became insane and his money is thought to be still buried somewhere in the Cove.

Another story tells of Pierre Perriau or Paddy Pierre as he was sometimes called. He was staying at the old Royal Hotel in Newcastle and was walking French Fort Cove when he encountered the nun who offered him money to find her head, but he fled in terror.

The nun, feeling that he might be a suitable person to find her missing head, apparently appeared to him in his sleep at the hotel that night. The next day he was so afraid that he left for Saint John.

Undaunted by the distance and so convinced that he could help her, the nun is reported to have visited him there. Pierre eventually left Saint John to live in Buffalo, New York, and the nun then returned to the Cove to haunt others, especially those who walked the bridge across Crow Brook along part of the old highway that ran from Bathurst through the Cove and Miramichi enroute to Fredericton.

In another story relating to French Fort Cove, McKay says that a group in the Cove community were having a card game one night when a "mysterious gentleman" approached them and asked if he might play.

The group said "yes" and the stranger began playing, and winning. It was obvious to the group that the stranger was cheating when a high card slipped from his sleeve and fell to the floor. The stranger then left immediately.

When the men reached down to pick up the fallen card, they saw a cloven hoof burnt into the floor. The mysterious man had been the devil!

There is also another story of a man walking French Fort Cove and being approached by "The Headless Nun". She apparently touched him in the back of the head, and where her three fingers touched, there were left three white patches of hair. The man is reported to have been constantly turning to look over his shoulder until he developed a twitching movement which drove him insane.

Today the French Fort Cove has been developed as a public walking and hiking area. With its steep terrain, beautiful trails and scenic lookouts, it provides an excellent recreational facility for the Miramichi.

It is said that the crows still gather at dusk near the bridge over Crow Brook at French Fort Cove to crow in memory of Sister Marie Inconnus.

So beware! If you are walking the French Fort Cove, particularly at night, and during a full moon, be careful! You may not be alone. You could be approached by any of the restless spirits which still haunt these lonely hills, or better still, by "The Headless Nun" herself.

The Headless Nun
by Doug Underhill

To the generations
Of those in Miramichi
There lives a legend
Of a headless nun.

Late one afternoon
Returning from her work
She walked the French Fort Cove
And not a sound was heard.

A mad man with brandished sword
And a mind gone rambling mad
Rushes from the forest and slashes her head
Leaving blood stains in the sand.

(Chorus)
She won't hurt you.
She's just alone.
She's just asking.
Make my body whole.

Next day they found her body
But no trace of her head.
They searched and searched but to no avail
A spirit without rest.

They laid her in the ground
In a grave across the sea
A headless body
A spirit never free.

(Chorus)

Far above the town
As the sun is going down
She walks the cove at night
Headless and alone.

She'll pay you plenty
Begging all who roam
To send her head
To send her head back home.

(Chorus)

She's just alone
.........just alone...

(Chorus)

Make my B-O-D-Y W-H-O-L-E
....oooooh.....ahaaaa..

(Chorus)

Headless Nun Halts A Horse

When Edmond Robichaud was 14 years old, he used to deliver mail from Newcastle to Mill Bank. The year was 1926 and the mail was delivered by horse and wagon. Edmond tells a story of a day when he was sick and his friend Joe Mullin had to take the reins. He starts out:

The old road he followed went through French Fort Cove across a log bridge back in the cove. On the way back to Newcastle at dusk, Mullin's horse came down the curve and crossed the bridge, but then stopped suddenly, turned around and went back.

Mullin turned the horse and came down the hill again to get some speed up for the hill on the other side of the bridge, but as the horse crossed the bridge it stopped again.

Halting horse in it's tracks!

Mullin went back even higher on the opposite hill and tried a third time. This time he had the horse at a gallop, but it stopped again a little way past the bridge.

Mullin tried to take the reins and lead the horse up the hill, but it refused to go any further. Finally, he had to return to Douglastown where he spent the night.

The next morning he brought another lad with him. After they had crossed the bridge and got to where the horse had stopped the previous night, the horse kept on without a stir, going right past where it had stopped three times the night before.

Mullin and his friend stopped the horse and went back to the spot where the horse had stopped the previous night. There they saw small footprints made by a lady's shoes.

Mullin had seen no one there the night before, and the footprints led nowhere. It was just as if someone had been standing in the spot.

"It had to be the Headless Nun", said Robichaud.

The Dungarvon Whooper

Probably the best known Miramichi ghost story is that of the Dungarvon Whooper. The story of the Whooper revolves around an alleged murder in a lumber camp in the woods near Whooper Springs along the Dungarvon River. When it actually took place is a matter of conjecture, and changes depending on the story teller, but it seems to

Dungarvon Whooper deep in the woods of the Miramichi.

have occurred somewhere between 1850 and 1875, although no concrete evidence has come to light.

The Dungarvon River is a tributary which flows into the Renous River about seven miles above Quarryville where the Renous empties into the main Southwest Miramichi.

Whooper Springs is located up the Dungarvon, but not actually on the river. It is in the area between the Renous-Plaster Rock Highway and back of Blackville. One reaches the area just above what locally is known as the "Black Swamp Road". Whooper Springs is then found below what is called "Dead Man's Spring".

Roy MacRae of Blackville said that the forestry service have placed a marker on the spot with Michael Whalen's poem encased in plastic. MacRae was called upon several years ago to conduct tours to the spot during a celebration of Miramichi Days.

The story of the Dungarvon Whooper was made famous by

Michael Whalen, "Poet of Renous", in his ballad titled "The Dungarvon Whooper" which first appeared around 1912.

As the story goes, a group of lumbermen were working the woods near Whooper Springs and when they came in for supper after their day's work, they found "the young cook silent, cold and dead".

When they questioned "the skipper", the only other person in the camp that day, "why he made no wild outcry", his reply was

> *"Well, the youngster took so sick,*
> *And he died so mighty quick,*
> *I hadn't time to think," was all he said.*

There apparently was no obvious evidence of a struggle or any other reason to suspect any wrong doing, but Whalen says in his poem

> *From his belt about his waist*
> *All his money was misplaced*
> *Which made the men suspect some serious wrong.*
> *Was it murder cold and dread*
> *That befell the fair young dead*
> *Where the dark and deep Dungarvon rolls along?*

The men then prepared the young cook for burial, but that night there came a very strong storm which prevented the men from taking the cook's remains back to the community for proper burial.

> *Fast fell the driven snow*
> *While the wild winds did blow*
> *Till four feet deep upon the ground it lay,*
> *So on the burial day*
> *To the graveyard far away*
> *To bear the corpse impossible was found.*

The lumbermen then had to bury the body in a shallow grave in the forest.

Then a forest grave was made
And in it the cook was laid
While the song birds and woodsmen ceased their song.

However, since the forest grave was unblessed, the body of the cook was unable to rest in peace. That night the camp and lumber-woods were subjected to such unearthly screams and whoops, that before dawn the hearty lumbermen were so afraid that they left the camp and refused to return to work in the area.

While the shades o' night were falling o'er the hill
All the long and fearful night
All the camp was in a fright,
Such fearful whoops and yells the forest fill
Pale and ghastly was each face
"We shall leave this fearful place
For this camp unto the demons does belong,
Ere the dawning of the day
We will hasten far away
From where the dark Dungarvon rolls along.

Stories tell that the lumbermen would not return to work the area as they and others heard terrible screams and whoops coming from the woods.

Since that day so goes the word
Fearful sounds have long been heard,
Far round the scene where lies the woodsman's grave
Whoops the stoutest hearts to thrill

Yells the warmest blood to chill
Sends terror to the bravest of the brave.

So real were the stories that Reverend Father Edward Murdock, the Roman Catholic parish priest at Renous, actually went up to the grave area of the Dungarvon and blessed the grave to quiet the restless spirit and free the area from its influence. Manny and Wilson say that Rev. Murdock actually "read the church service of exorcism," but apparently, there is no official record of him doing so in the church records.

Till beside the grave did stand
God's good man with lifted hand
And prayed that He those sounds should not prolong
And that the region rest in peace
Where the deep Dungarvon sweeps along.

Whalen's poem says that it was reported that the blessing worked as the whoops and yells ceased and the region was at peace.

Since that day the sounds have ceased
And the region is released
From those unearthly whoops and screams and yells
All around the Whooper's spring
There is heard no evil thing
And round the Whooper's grave sweet silence dwells.

However, people still say that they have heard the wild shrieks and yells and that the area remains haunted.

In the book *Songs of Miramichi* Dr. Louise Manny and James Reginald Wilson say that:

"Possibly the awful shrieks had often been heard in the woods before the alleged murder of the cook, and were those of a screech owl, or those of a panther. However, the story of a murder made a most satisfactory explanation, and other bits of folklore have been added to the tale, like filings to a magnet".

They say that the tale now has "among its attributes ever-blooming flowers on the grave, a ghost which rises screaming if the grave is disturbed, a feu follet type of apparition, or rather sound, which entices the hearer into the woods, where he is lost, or sometimes lures him with the smell of frying bacon, or a shrieking spectre which comes nearer and nearer to the unlucky person who answers the sounds. Finally, ...the scream is heard directly over the answerer , in the open air, and he is too terrified to answer it again".

The name "Dungarvon" comes from Ireland and probably brings with it a good deal of the Irish folklore such as the screams of the banshee which would give the basis of the Whooper story.

Whatever the truth to the tales, the story has persevered and today is accepted as the most famous of the ghost stories on the Miramichi. So famous has it become, that it had a train, and eventually a tavern, named after it.

There was a train which ran from Quarryville (then called Indiantown) to Newcastle. It carried the crowds of woodsmen who were whooping it up with songs and fun, and most likely a drop or two.

Every time the train approached a station or siding stop, they would whoop in chorus to the whistle of the train. A curious spectator at the station in Newcastle asked CNR conductor Edward S. Vye what train this was and he replied "The Dungarvon Whooper".

The name stuck and was given to the train which ran from Fredericton to Newcastle. The eerie sound of the steam locomotive's whistle was a natural fit to the legend of the Whooper's screams.

The actual "Whooper" made its last train run on Friday, April 24,1936 according to Manny and Wilson. A passenger aboard the train was Conductor Vye who was in charge of the inaugural run and the person responsible for giving the train the fame of its name.

Subsequently, when a tavern was opened in the old Chatham railway station in the 1970's, it combined the legend of the train and the story of "The Dungarvon Whooper" and was known as "The Whooper".

Ralph Thompson Encounters The Great Whooper

With all the fame of the Dungarvon Whooper, there have been many attempts to explain what the Whooper actually is. Some have said it was a ghost and others a panther screaming, but Ralph Thompson knows. He encountered the Whooper about 1975. He picks up the story:

"I was hunting bobcats up the Dungarvon Road. It was about 10:00 p.m. at night and I was trying to catch my dog. I had driven my ski-doo back down the road to the Whooper Spring. I could hear my dog coming through the swamp chasing a cat, so I walked in to cut him off."

"I was being very quiet so as not to turn the cat. I put my flashlight out and waited. That's when I found out what the Dungarvon Whooper was."

"He let out two or three whoops. They were whoops and not screams. They were identical to a man whooping. If I hadn't been where I was, I'd have been out

Encountering
The Dungarvon Whooper.

of there, but they came from a tree right over my head. It was a bird."

"I told others about what I had heard, but no one believed me except Archie Jardine. He was a boat builder from the Rapids. He'd trapped that area for years."

"I told him I knew what the Dungarvon Whooper was and he said, 'So do I'. So I said, 'What is it ?', and he said, 'An Owl'. I knew it was a bird, but not an owl. Jardine knew it was an owl, but didn't know what type, but he had heard it down in that same swamp over the years. He said that he had trapped a lot of country, but had never heard the same sound anywhere else except in that swamp. If you heard it, you would know why people think it is a man. It would scare people, but I assure you there were no tracks around the tree."

The Friendly Ghost of Murray House

One of the newer ghost stories in the Miramichi is "The Ghost of Murray House". The Murray house is an historic home built by William Murray in 1825, and recently restored to its original form and placed at Ritchie Wharf in the former town of Newcastle in Miramichi.

Murray was one of Miramichi's famed builders who came from Scotland around 1825. He left his distinct style of architecture on many of Miramichi's famous buildings such as the Miramichi Golf Club, The Rankin House in Douglastown, the Court House in Newcastle, St. James Presbyterian Church (now the St James - St. John United Church) in Newcastle, the Samuel House in Chatham, The United Church in Blackville, St. Peter's in Bartibogue, the cupola of the Seamen's Hospital in Douglastown, the Goodfellow house in South Esk, the old court house across from St. James in Newcastle, the Williston House in Newcastle and of course his own cottage house today known as "The Murray House".

The actual Murray house was built about 1826 by Murray himself while he was working on St. James Church. It and a workshop were built on a lot next to the church where it remained until 1918 when it was moved to the Stothart property adjacent to the church. At the time the cottage was moved it was owned by Miss Sarah Murray, a grand daughter of Murray, and her nephew George M. Lake.

When it had to be moved again, it came into the hands of the Gray family who lived on Prince William Street in Newcastle. The Murray House was relocated behind the Court House in

Murray House at Ritchie Wharf in Newcastle.

the Gray's back yard. Mrs. Gray was a relative of the Murray family and so the house stayed in the family.

In 1974 the house was listed as being owned by J. Alexander (Lucky) Gray. The house stayed in this location until it was sold to the provincial government. They in turn gave it to the historical society to be moved to Ritchie Wharf where it was restored to its original state.

Over the years the roof had been altered and a glass porch added to the front, but the cottage was restored to its original state when it was placed at Ritchie Wharf.

Bobby Gray, a son of Lucky Gray, said that the family did not want to sell the house and even considered selling one of their own houses and moving into it. But when they heard it would be restored and preserved for future generations, they agreed.

Bobby said that his father loved the cottage and certainly spent a lot of time in it, and the family was happy to see it where it is now. Little did the family realize, but the spirit of Lucky Gray may also have been pleased with the new location.

It was during the restoration at Ritchie Wharf that the story of its ghost first was told. Fred Adair, an employee with the Ritchie Wharf Shipbuilding Commission, who serves as caretaker of the Ritchie Wharf tourist area, was the first to tell the tale of "The Ghost of Murray House".

Reconstruction had taken place during the summer and fall with most of the windows being boarded up for the winter. However, the power had been left on to preserve the renovations and contents of the house. It had snowed heavily and there were no tracks leading into the building.

As Adair was working at the Wharf he would often see a gentleman from Africa who had emigrated to the Miramichi via England. Everyday this gentleman would come to the ploughed parking area of Ritchie Wharf to walk his dog.

One day he approached Adair and asked who was living in The Murray House. Adair told him that no one was living there as it had been closed for the winter.

The gentleman was insistent that someone was living there and told Adair about seeing a man sitting in the window with a dog in his lap.

Adair declared that he must have been mistaken as there was definitely no one living in the house. The man became rather indignant and told Adair that there was definitely someone there and he had seen him with his dog sitting in his lap almost every day when he came to walk his own dog.

Adair pointed out that there were no tracks in the snow and no paths shoveled and that the place was not being used by anyone. The man left angry and still convinced he had seen someone.

That spring when some of Lucky Gray's relatives were visiting the area, they requested that Adair take them on a tour of the house even though it had not been completely restored.

When Adair was leading them through the house one of the ladies said, "I can still see Lucky sitting there by the window with his little dog in his lap".

"When she said that I could feel the shivers going up my back. When I told her the story of the man walking his dog, we both stood there in awe," said Adair. In another incident related by Adair, he had gone upstairs after the renovations were completed.

"All the gyprock and dust had settled and there was a pile of dirt swept up lying on the floor, and in the dust on the floor there were obvious dog tracks all around it. No one had been going in or out of the building all winter because I was the only one with a key and I don't have a dog. You explain it to me," said Adair.

Adair also told of a conversation with one of the security guards who knew nothing of the above story. The guard off handedly told him he thought The Murray House was haunted.

"He mentioned hearing footsteps and noises in the fall, and as a result he would not stay there, preferring to work out of the wash-room area instead," said Adair.

"The Ghost of Murray House," is obviously a friendly ghost because it has done no harm to anybody or anything. Since Lucky Gray always loved the old cottage and spent a lot of time in it, maybe he is still keeping an eye on it as he sits by his window with his little dog in his lap. If that is so, "The Murray House" is still in very good hands.

The Ghost of Murray House sitting
in the window.

The Ghost Who Wanted His Bill Paid

An interesting ghost story comes from a priest who is a friend of mine. He told me the story of a ghost who wanted to make sure his bill had been paid.

Father Burns, a priest at Renous, had told him the story which took place some time in the 1930's.

The story is about a man named Johnny who came up to Blackville to have his watch fixed. When he returned to get his watch, he told the repairman that he did not have the money to pay him at that moment.

The repairman was very obliging and said that it was "OK" and for him to pay him the next time he was in town.

As fate would have it, the man died before he was able to return to pay for his watch being repaired.

Some time later, Johnny's ghost appeared to the repairman while he was awake, and told him to go to his wife to collect for the repairs. His spirit would not rest until his bill had been paid. The skeptics would probably say this is a tale about a creative bill collector rather than a ghost.

The Spectre Who Stopped A Wagon

Father Vincent Donovan of Renous told a story of his great grandfather John Donovan who was returning from Fredericton by wagon sometime in the mid 1860's.

When he reached Quarryville and turned up the road to Renous near Billy Hawkes' place, the wagon stopped and the horse refused to go any further. Donovan's grandfather has always maintained that he saw a ghostly light on the road that spooked the horse.

Whether this occurrence was a ghost or merely the presence of swamp gas which is sometimes common along the flats near the river is unknown.

Father Donovan laughed as he hypothesized that the wagon was probably never greased and had just seized after the long trip.

Joe Augustine's Spooky Tales

It would seem the ghosts of the Miramichi were also a part of the Native community's folklore as well.

Madeline Augustine has provided the following stories which she collected from her grandfather Joe Augustine.

Joe Augustine was responsible for discovering The Augustine Mound (named after him) and The Oxbow, two national historic sites of the Red Bank Micmac Natives. These discoveries enabled the Micmacs to trace their roots on the Miramichi back some 3,000 years and established Red Bank as the oldest community in the province.

Augustine's life was subsequently made into a documentary which traced his archaeological discoveries.

Madeline tells this story about her famous grandfather. Joe had many ghost and witch stories. Apparently, there was this one ghost which was quite popular over eighty years ago, in the time of his grandfather, Sam Augustine.

This ghost was a tall woman with eyes you could not see. She had only two black holes which seemed to stare right through you. She was never seen without her long white robe and a black scarf which was always wrapped around her head.

"In them olden times," grandfather would start off, signalling to everyone that a story was to follow, "Indians would go up into the woods to get ash to make baskets".

"One time when my grandfather was about seventeen or eighteen, he went up somewhere near Salmon River Road with three older fellows to get ash, eh. They were staying in one of those shacks near the railroad, and they didn't get back until late in the evening."

"Grandfather went on to describe the night as very bright as it was a full moon night. He also described one of the fellows in the group as one with a lot of nerve and the strongest in the crowd."

"As they were approaching the camp, they could see a woman standing over the hill. She was wearing a long white robe and they could see black around her head."

"Upon realizing that she was a ghost, the tough guy spoke first".

"Boys," he said, "If anyone comes with me I can go over there and touch that ghost."

"Nobody spoke up so it was Sam who said he would go with him".

"As they approached the ghost, Sam noticed a stick laying on the ground and picked it up. They were about ten feet away when the tough fellow would not go any further."

"They could see the ghost standing up. She was a woman with great big eyes. They looked to be like holes right through her eyes, you know, black holes grandfather described to me."

He continued:

"He wouldn't go any closer. Scared, eh?. It was then that Sam stood back and with stick in hand, took a swing at the ghost, knocking her to the ground."

"The ghost, unphased by the assault, jumped back up and went after the four men. They started running towards the open door of the camp, with Sam being the fastest of them all."

"It took four strong men to hold that door closed. They could feel the powerful force pulling from behind the door. On the door was once a window now covered with shingles."

"This ghost was strong and at last she put her head right through the shingles," said Augustine using his grandfather's words.

"Sam then grabbed a large poker which was sitting by the door and proceeded to hit the ghost over the head. He gave the ghost four or five solid whacks before the ghost pulled back out of the window, falling to the ground."

"Nobody could sleep all night as they recounted over and over again their frightening experience with the ghost."

"By morning, the three older gentlemen had fallen asleep. Sam got up and opened the door, carefully peeking his head out to investigate the scene."

"At the bottom of his feet he saw a large stump laying on the ground, measuring about six feet long and about twelve inches in diameter. On the top of the stump , Sam could see four or five heavy marks, the result of a pounding of some heavy object."

"You see, the ghost had turned into a stump," grandfather explained. "And this is a true story. It happened many, many times, you know."

"It also happened to my uncle Bill-William Augustine from Big Cove," grandfather said.

"He was coming from some neighbours in Big Cove when he came up to this brook. He was thirsty so he laid down to have a drink of water. All of a sudden, a ghost, the same one, was standing about thirty feet away from him," grandfather recounted.

"He didn't know what to do, so he picked up a rock, about the size of an egg and pelted it at the ghost. He hit it, knocked it down and then ran home."

"The next day, Bill returned to the brook. Laying in the same location where the ghost had stood was a tree stump. Closer to the top was a woodpecker hole with a rock lodged inside of it. It was the same ghost again," explained grandfather. "Uncle Bill had seen her too!"

The Spooked Ghost

The following is another native ghost story collected by Madeline Augustine.
Ghost stories were quite popular among native elders of the mi'qmaq. Many of the ones told to me contained a strong element of humour. Perhaps this is the reason why the old Indians were never

afraid of ghosts or spirits.

John Peter Augustine was another elder in the community of Red Bank. He passed away in 1989. After eight or nine years of residential schooling at Shubenacadie, N.S., John returned to the community of Red Bank, unable to speak his native tongue. In 1978 John Peter participated in a project entitled the "Red Bank History Project".

Here, John Peter recounts the days of living with his uncle/caretaker, Joe Augustine, and some of the ghost stories old Joe had told him.

"In olden times the old time Indians made their own snowshoes and everyone would walk back and forth to the sugary. In those times they only had little wigwams where they could build little fires inside with a hole on top to let the smoke out."

"So this one afternoon, just about when it was getting dark, this old Indian was walking toward the sugary. When he got handy to the sugary, he thought he heard something. He turned around and there was this ghost following him. So he waited for him and he and the ghost had a little conversation as they walked to the sugary."

"When they got handy to the sugary, this ghost stopped and wouldn't go any further. So, the Indian chap stopped and asked the ghost what was the matter."

"The ghost told him `You know what, I'm scared of that strange ghost way over there.' (laughing) One ghost was scared of another. Old Joe told me that one."

Phantom By The Roadside

I was told the following story by Ray Estey when I was in high school. My father Clarence and I used to visit his hunting camp on the Sevogle River. Ray Estey and his brother Frank were well known folk singers and story tellers from Sevogle. They were regular performers at the annual Miramichi Folk Song Festival. Ray's son Edward helped me with details of the story.

Ray Estey said that he was driving a horse and sleigh at the time of the story. It was a full moon night in 1928 when he was about 40 years old. He was near Shaddick's Store in Trout Brook .

Spectre of a young girl halts horse and wagon.

He was coming down the road when he saw a young girl standing along the side of the road.

"I'm going down the road so you might as well get in and come along," said Estey, but she didn't move a muscle.

"I asked her a second time and she still didn't move, so I asked her a third time. Then she opened her mouth and showed every tooth in her head. It looked like she was the devil," said Ray.

Estey said that he was so scared that he couldn't speak. He had a fast horse, so he kicked at the whip and the horse jumped and took off. When he turned his head to look back, there was no one there.

When he got home he began to calm down and put together the details of the scene. He remembered that there had been a little snow on the ground, and when he thought about the girl standing by the side of the road, he could see her standing about two or three inches above the snow with not a footprint visible.

Estey then told his story to his mother. When she heard the story she said, "Why, that's Irene Copp. She died twenty years ago".

Light In The Graveyard

One of the more popular ghost stories from the Loggieville area is the story of the "Light in the Graveyard".

The graveyard in question is the Pine Grove Cemetery located on what was called the back road to Loggieville. Now it is the road that leads from "Taintville" to Loggieville.

When driving by the graveyard at night there seemed to be a reflection or weird light coming off of one of the headstones. Whether it was a reflection from a street light on the river road to Loggieville, moonlight, or an actual supernatural occurrence from the spirit world, is hard to say. But its presence is widely known.

Many a young man would take his girlfriend along the back road and hope that the light in the graveyard could be seen. If it was, frequently it would propel the lady closer to the guy. This in itself was reason enough to perpetuate the story.

One gentleman said that the reason for the mystery was that the grave held a Catholic soul in a Protestant Cemetery.

Perhaps added to this is another ghost story from Loggieville. On summer nights, many of the local boys would often sleep out for the night. There was a rumour about an old man who would walk the streets continually at night.

The boys in the tent would hear the footsteps along the same back road of Loggieville that was haunted by the light in the graveyard. They would crawl from the tent into the ditch to see if they could see who this man was, but when they would get there, there would be no one in sight. This apparently happened many times.

Whether the two are related, can only be answered by the powers beyond.

The Spirit of Sheleighah Cove

Another interesting ghost in the Miramichi is the "Ghost of Sheleighah Cove". Sheleighah Cove is located about five miles below Red Bank on the Northwest branch of the Miramichi River on the western side of the river.

The story revolves around Richard McLaughlin, an Irish immigrant who became a local businessman who operated one of the main lumbering businesses in the Red Bank area in 1825. He held a host of public offices such as commissioner of highways, school trustee, grand juror, and member of the Northwest Boom committee.

The Great Miramichi Fire of 1825 left McLaughlin with severe losses from which he never recovered. It was said that he owed Alexander Rankin of Douglastown huge amounts of money which he paid and then sold the remainder of his possessions at a public auction in 1828 to try to pay off Joseph Cunard.

As the story goes, he had gone to Newcastle by scow, going down with the tide. Upon his return he was as far as Sheleighah Cove when the tide changed, so he put ashore to rest.

While there, he received word that there were creditors looking for him, so by moonlight he dumped his gold coins into the cove, hoping to return later to retrieve them. However, he died before he was able to do so.

After his death there were reports that on the night of every full moon, there was a man in a scow at Sheleighah Cove looking for his treasure.

If You See A Ghost, Close Your Eyes and Drive Right Through It

The story of "The Ghost of Sheleighah Cove" was well known and has an amusing story related to it thanks to some advice from Art MacTavish.

MacTavish had heard of many encounters with the Ghost of Sheleighah Cove. At the Cove there was a steep hill.

MacTavish was telling stories, and apparently told a group of friends what to do if they ever encountered a ghost. He said that since they could not grab a ghost or push it away, the only answer was to go right through it.

One night, Art's nephew Billy MacTavish was coming home from his girlfriend's house in Red Bank. He had told his father he would be home before dark, but he was a little late.

He was driving a bicycle, and since he was late, he was going pretty fast. It was getting dark and it was hard to see. When he came to the top of Sheleighah Hill, he saw something white at the bottom.

He remembered what his uncle had told him about going through the ghost, and closed his eyes and peddled as fast as he could.

The white ghost turned out to be a cow and he ran right into it. He broke his bike, but did not seem to do any damage to the cow.

Look out! It's not a ghost... it's a cow!

The Haunting of Hierlihy Road

The following story was provided by Stanley MacDonald, and is best told in his own words.

For many years the Hierlihy Road in Northumberland County served as a vital artery between the communities of Tabusintac and Price Settlement. It served as a portage road which linked other communities nearby, providing an alternative to river travel.

In the early 1900's it was once a busy route joining roadside homesteads to one another, but today its residents are elegant pine and stately birch trees.

It was upon this Hierlihy Road that a Mr. William Savoy trod afoot one cool crisp autumn evening many years ago. As the tale goes, after completing the chores and having filled the woodbox for the next day, he was on his way to pay a call to his sweetheart.

As Mr. Savoy came in sight of a spot commonly known as "Mill Hill," he noticed a dense haze somewhat like a fog lying at the

Mr. Savoy yelling to the ghost traveller.

foot of the slope. As he drew near to the fog, he could hear the approaching sound of a horse and wagon.

After another moment or two, he noticed a somewhat tired looking steed emerging from the mist, drawing behind her what appeared by sight and sound to be a peddler's cart.

Upon the seat of the buckboard sat an aged man dressed in sombre black with a broad rimmed hat and shoulders rounded from a life time of labour and toil.

Stepping aside to allow the wagon passage, Mr. Savoy twice yelled a greeting to the night time traveller, but got no response. The only sound to be heard in the night was the steady creaking of the wagon and the clanging of pots and pans as it passed by.

Then just as mysteriously as it had appeared, the wagon, wares and driver were swallowed up again in a cloud of fog not 20 feet beyond where it had passed our friend.

When this story was recounted the next day at home, Mr. Savoy was to hear from his father that many years previous a very respected mercantile agent enroute from Cains Point to Tabusintac had suffered an ambush and lost his life while crossing the brook at the foot of Mill Hill.

It was said that the next day a number of men from the near-by settlement buried the dead peddler's horse in the woods at the foot of the hill. The horse had been shot by a stray bullet, but no sign of injury could be found on the body of the old gentleman. It was felt by the locals that since there was no money found on the old man's body, that he had fallen among thieves.

Mr. Savoy lived out a long and full life in Tabusintac as a well respected neighbour and friend to all. However, he vowed, regardless of circumstances, he would never again walk that stretch of road alone, and to the best of my knowledge, he never did.

The Wailing Child in the Walls

One interesting ghost story involves the F. P. Loggie house in the former Loggieville. Frank P. Loggie and his brothers Andrew and Robert were three brothers who ran a company known as A & R Loggie. During the late 1800s and first part of the 1900s the three controlled a network of stores, owned a saw mill and were into the fishing business, shipping their products far and wide. They all had huge houses in Loggieville on the front street facing the Miramichi River. This story involves the large two story F. P. Loggie house.

Theresa Kelly of Loggieville has often heard a child crying in the walls of the old F. P. Loggie house in Loggieville, now part of the City of Miramichi.

Kelly said that she had lived in the Loggie house for about five years in the early 1960s. It was during this time that she could hear strange wailings coming from within the walls.

Child crying in the walls of the F.P. Loggie house.

"I would often hear what sounded like a baby crying from the walls in the back stairs area. One morning a friend of mine named Doris McGrath came down the stairs and I told her she looked terrible. She said that of course she did because she had been kept awake all night by my baby crying. I told her that my baby had slept through. It was the crying coming from the wall that she heard."

Her mother Bea Murdock always felt that the house was haunted and would never stay there alone.

Kelly also told of another time when her husband was away on business. He had phoned to say he would not be home because of a snowstorm. She was by herself and got up to feed the baby about 2:00 a.m..

"When I came into the kitchen, the cupboards were rattling. I knew there was nothing unusual in them as I had just cleaned them that day. I hollered 'stop your rattling because you don't scare me' and it stopped. Then I began to get scared," said Kelly.

"Another time we had friends visiting. The men were in the inside room while one of the ladies was in the kitchen with me. We had put the kids to bed and were talking, when her husband came out to ask why the children were crying. We had just checked them and they were asleep, so I told them about the baby crying in the wall. That's what they were hearing. They looked shocked," she recalled.

"I have heard stories of others after we moved who said that they had seen a man in the garage, but I never saw anything like that. For me it was mostly the baby crying in the walls. I wasn't really scared because you kind of get used to it. But I was glad when we moved," said Kelly.

The Hauntings of Allan Kelly

Allan Kelly spent a good part of his life in lumber camps cutting logs, tending store and being a school trustee, but he is perhaps best known for his folk songs and his record of never having missed singing in a Miramichi Folk Song Festival in 41 years. At age 95 he is still sharp as the axes he used in the woods.

Born in Pointe Sapin near Baie Ste. Anne, N.B. Kelly was one of 13 in the family of 11 boys and two girls.

"It was hard to raise a family because we didn't have a lot of money, so I was raised by the Robichaud family in Pointe Sapin. They were rich people in those days. They were kind and looked after me. That's where I learned to speak French because everyone there only spoke French. The only English I heard was when my dad would visit on Sundays," said Kelly.

Kelly went to work in the lumber camps when he was 16 years old, and sawed logs with his brother Ed.

"We sawed together with an old cross cut saw. We cut between 100 to 105 logs a day. We always kept a few back for a rainy day. The last day of the season we turned in 140 logs. I worked at that until I quit in 1930 and took a 100 acre grant and did a lot of the clearing of it myself

because I was too poor to hire anyone else. I didn't own a horse, so I raised a great big bull to do the work and trained him for the yoke. I raised 11 kids cutting my own wood, railroad ties, and veneer wood. I also cleared some ground to plant a bit."

Kelly worked for Bill McCombs who used to buy wood from him for a Swedish company.

"They found me honest I guess because they hired me to work for them buying their wood for 15 years. Then in 1950 I bought a store on the road to Belfont and operated it for 21 years. I had no education, having left school in grade two, but I became

Alan Kelly

an overseer of the poor, a school trustee and a singer in the church choir for 15 years in Beaverbrook. I kept the store until I retired to Elmwood Lane. I guess I'll remain here because I'm too old to travel," said Kelly.

Besides having a repertoire of over 100 folk songs which he sings in both French and English, Kelly has never sung the same song twice while performing in all 41 years of the Miramichi Folksong Festival. There are 90 tapes of his songs at the Université de Moncton, and he has his own album of songs.

But besides his songs, Kelly had some very good ghost stories.

"I didn't believe in ghost stories, but when it happened to me I had to believe," said Allan Kelly.

"My brother Tom and I were fishing spring herring in Tabusintac in 1925, a year after I was married. The W. S. Loggie Company had a factory on the beach where they kept their ropes and traps for the winter, and they kept it closed with a padlock and chain."

"In spring around ice out about April 15 we'd set our nets for catching herring when there came up a Northeast storm. We had built a camp of seaweed and sticks to stay in, but the wind blew the seaweed off, and with the wind and rain coming in, we were wet and cold. We had no where to go, so we took a hatchet and broke into the W. S. Loggie factory."

"We went in and laid on the coils of rope and weren't down more than five to ten minutes when there was a noise. There was a set of stairs to the second floor so we went up, but there was no one there. But we could hear chains rattling. We couldn't stand it. We had to leave. There was something strange going on, so we had to cross the bay by canoe to a sports camp to stay the night. It was a long ten mile row, but it was worth it rather than staying there with whatever was rattling those chains. What could have happened in the past to start those chains rattling?"

Kelly's repertoire of ghost stories include the following tale:

"Frasers had an old mill across the Morrissy Bridge from Newcastle in the Chatham Head area. We worked there all summer. A guy from Tracadie ran a boarding house in Newcastle charging thirty-five cents a meal in those days. There were 14 of us at the old boarding house. The company had four or five houses near to the mill, and my brother Edmond wanted one so we moved over into one of them that was empty in the fall," said Kelly.

"They told us we would never stay there because the house was haunted, but we moved there. The house was all one room with no divider. One night, we didn't go to work. I was sleeping by the stairs. It was after midnight and Ed was snoring when I heard something coming. It sounded like a herd of cattle outside."

"Then something broke the door. The house was shaking. Something sounding like a horse went by me, blew in my face and went right up the stairs. I tried to wake Edmond and his wife, but they wouldn't wake up."

"The next morning when I told them, they wouldn't believe me. They said it was a dream or nightmare. Good enough," I said.

"The next night Edmond heard it. He had a book of matches and tried to light one, but it wouldn't stay lit. They couldn't wake me this time. His wife was so scared that we moved out the next day and went to Newcastle and we never went back."

"After we moved out, there was an older man and woman who lived in the same house. They didn't stay too long either. She was out one evening to get a pail of water from the spring. She fainted because she saw a man with no head who told her to come back at 12:00 a.m. sharp and there would be a fortune for her. She didn't go back, but she was never the same again."

Allan Kelly also tells a story about being his own ghost.

"It was one time I was out fishing eels with a canoe. We had an old fashioned lamp hung on the bow of the boat to attract the eels. Just coming on dark my wife had a lunch ready for us as we would come back at dark. She saw me coming up the lane with the lighted lamp. She thought she saw me put the lighted lamp down on the ground and figured I had gone back as I had forgotten something. She waited 15 minutes and no Allan."

"That same night, I had taken a turn while in the boat and almost drowned in the canoe. The young fellow with me couldn't fish, so he was paddling while I was watching and fishing. Seeing the seaweed made me dizzy. I drove my spear into the mud to stop from spinning. Then he made for shore, and I came to just as the boat hit shore. The young fellow kept me from falling into the channel."

"I guess the fellow with the lamp was my forerunner, someone sent ahead to warn us about something terrible about to happen. I guess he put the lamp down and did not go all the way to my house because my time was not up then."

According to Allan Kelly a forerunner was responsible for saving his life when he was lobster fishing.

"I was fishing lobster with my brother Edmond. He had a shanty for him and his wife, but I boarded in the cookhouse. I always slept in the top bunk. One night as it was coming on morning, I heard a bang on the roof and thought it was coming down. Talk about a noise, but it didn't wake the others. They were snoring like hell. It didn't bother me too much, and I went back to sleep."

"We'd get up at 6:00 a.m. and Edmond would drop over to get me. But for some reason, I didn't feel like going out that day. He wondered why because we didn't have a lot of money and we were paid about a dollar a day. He said he couldn't go alone, but I said that there was something telling me not to go out."

"There was a guy who lived close who was fishing herring, so he got him to go out with him. I went home to my father-in-law's house in Tracadie and told my wife something told me not to go out that day," recalled Kelly.

"During that day, the weather turned and we had a big Norwester. The bay was really rough. When the boats came in, Ed and the herring guy were the last ones in. To go ashore from the boats they used a small canoe. There were four guys in it already, and still Ed and the other guy to come."

"The other guys didn't want to make two trips so they tried to put six in the canoe. When Ed got in, it upset and one guy drowned. Ed said it could have been me. I guess the thump on the roof was a forerunner. When I told my wife what had happened, she said, 'Thank God you came home.' Before that I never believed those stories about forerunners. That's the truth, no lies," said Kelly.

"My brother-in-law was the same type of guy. He didn't believe in any of these stories. He lived in Tracadie. There was a path from the village to the store. He was going out with a girl and used the path to go and see her."

"One night in the fall of the year, he was coming home. It was a full moon that night. He heard a noise in the woods and turned back and saw six guys carrying a casket across the path. He didn't take that path again."

"I heard another story from my father, and he wouldn't tell a lie. If anyone told a lie, he would get the razor strap. There was an old log on the beach at Pointe Sapin. I used to sit on it a lot. My mother had died a while before. Then my father told me that he had seen my mother sitting on it all dressed in white. He started walking toward her, but she disappeared. Maybe she didn't want to scare him."

Kelly said that he had heard the story of the Dungarvon Whooper and had worked in the woods on the Dungarvon River.

"I drove that stream one spring. It was a rough stream to drive. When I was there, there was a hand-made wooden cross on the grave where he was buried. I saw the cross, but I never heard the "Whooper", but the guys at the lumber camp wouldn't go out alone at night. If you had to go out you had to get two or three together."

Ghost Stories

Folklore

Monsignor Ryan: Priest and Folk Healer

From the early 1920's to the mid 1950's, if anyone on the Miramichi had a peculiar medical problem, the question most likely asked was "Did you go to see Monsignor Ryan"?

Monsignor Ryan was well known on the Miramichi and beyond as a "folk healer". His cures and concoctions were literally legendary. He had cures like straw baths, wraps from boiled pine needles, special tonics, and a host of other unusual remedies for many ailments.

Being a priest would naturally instill a certain faith in him by those who knew him, and this probably added to the effectiveness of his cures.

Monsignor Ryan was born in Kouchibouguac, New Brunswick on January 18, 1876, the son of Patrick Ryan and Ann Donovan. He studied at St. Joseph University and Holy Heart Seminary in Halifax, Nova Scotia and was ordained a priest by Bishop Barry in Chatham, N.B. on July 17, 1904.

He spent a year in Tracadie, N.B. and then was transferred to Tobique Missions above Perth-Andover, N.B. on the St. John River. He remained there from 1905 until 1921. It was probably here working with the natives on the Tobique Reserve that he learned many of his folk and herbal cures.

In 1921 he was appointed to the parish of Red Bank, N.B. on the Northwest Miramichi as Pastor of St. Thomas parish where he remained until 1955 at which time he retired. He then spent his last years at Mount St. Joseph in Chatham, N.B. where he died May 9, 1973.

Folklore

Monsignor Ryan is buried in St. Michael's Cemetery in the former Chatham, N.B.

He was described as a gentleman outside, but fiery on the inside. Some of the parishioners who knew him found him to be a very stern man who would put up with no foolishness. His sermons were often long and scathing if the situation warranted it. He was not a man to mince words. He frowned upon dancing and told his congregation pointedly.

It is reported that when a couple of men came to rob him when he was quite old, he actually threw one of them out of his house through a plate glass window.

Father Henry McGrath knew Monsignor Ryan well and was cured by him.

"He was a very interesting man. I had the pleasure of knowing him as one of his patients as well as a fellow priest. I remember going up to Red Bank to fill in for him one weekend. It was a nice early summer day and I did not arrive until about nine in the evening. He had gone to bed as he thought I was not coming. He was also an early riser, getting up about six," said McGrath.

McGrath said that Ryan did get up to meet him that evening, but went directly back to bed. The next morning Ryan gave McGrath his instructions for the Sunday service.

"He told me to sit down and told me that I probably wouldn't get done all that he did. He would start services at 9:00 a.m. and they would run until noon. He would begin with the Way of the Cross, then the rosary, give them a talk before mass, start mass, preach an hour-long sermon and finish off with the Benediction. He told me that since he only saw them once a week, he wanted to do all he could for them," said McGrath.

Yet, he was revered for the cures he brought to so many people. His fame was so widely known that many famous people came to him for his help. There are stories that he even treated singer Johnny Cash.

It was said that Monsignor Ryan was also very good friends with some German doctors and may have learned some of his cures from them.

McGrath remembered his first visit to Ryan. It was in 1935. McGrath was a sophomore at St. Thomas in Chatham and had been hurt playing basketball.

"The doctors operated on me and I spent the winter in bed without any improvement. The doctors did not know if I had a punctured stomach, a bad appendix, or tuberculosis of the bowel. So my parents called Monsignor Ryan. He said to be there at 2:00 p.m. sharp. And he meant it. He was a very busy man."

McGrath said that the first thing Ryan asked him was "Why weren't you here before?", and then before I could answer, "What did they (the doctors) say it was?", When I told him the three options, his reply was "You don't have any of that. I can tell by looking at you. I'm putting you on pine packs", said McGrath.

McGrath took the pine pack treatment which consisted of gathering large quantities of pine needles and then boiling them in water, "which became a dirty brown colour". After the liquid cooled, it was necessary to soak a sheet in the liquid and then wrap the body in the wet sheet every two hours.

"It was very cold when you first wrapped yourself in it, but gradually you would warm up. I had to do this for a month. I went back after a month and he cut the wraps down to twice a day, and then after a while told me I could stop, but that I had to eat raw liver which I did with it being cut up very small. He also told me to eat a lot of raw tomatoes. Whatever it was, it worked because it cured me and a lot of others."

McGrath's aunt was having a problem with her throat, and they thought it might have been cancer, so she was sent to Monsignor Ryan who gave her peroxide to drink.

"It worked, but I certainly wouldn't recommend it to anybody," said McGrath.

It was believed that the doctors of the time tried to bring lawsuits against Ryan to stop him from meddling in the medical field, but since Ryan never charged anyone for helping them, there was nothing they could do legally.

McGrath still takes a daily tonic prescribed by Monsignor Ryan. The ingredients are as follows:

Father Ryan's Tonic (for general health)

Break 6 eggs (shells and all) in a dish. Break shells the size of a cent. Squeeze out the juice from 12 lemons (less if they are really big) (1 1/2 to 2 cups of juice) and pour over broken eggs.

Let stand 24 hours, stirring occasionally. Strain all through a course wire strainer.

Into this liquid add 1/2 pint (one cup) of cod liver oil, 1/2 pint (one cup) of bee's honey, 3/4 of a pint of Old Jamaica Rum (or other kind).

It is now ready for use. Shake well before using. Keep corked in a cool dry place. Take 2 or 3 teaspoons before meals.

Father Ryan's Arthritis Medicine

3 grapefruits
3 oranges
3 lemons

Extract juice from fruit (Store in fridge)
Put skins of grapefruit, oranges and lemons through a meat grinder
Pour over this one quart of boiling water
Let stand over night
Strain in morning
Mix with juices from fruit.

In another bowl put:
Two heaping teaspoons of Epsom Salts

3 tablespoons of Cream of Tarter
Add one pint of boiling water, stir well until dissolved
Add to fruit juices
Keep in fridge
Take one wine glass each morning before breakfast.

Another of Ryan's cures was for Eczema.
It went as follows:

Take five pounds of oat straw. Remove all the grains of oats and use only the straw.

Cut up in five or six inches in length and put all in a tin boiler and then pour on 1 1/2 pails of boiling water. Cover the boiler, shove to the back of the stove and steep for one hour. Do not boil.

Save the straw liquid. Use COLD or LUKEWARM.

Rule:

The longer and more often all parts that are covered with Eczema are soaked under this straw liquid, the quicker will be the cure.

Therefore, all day and everyday, soak sores under this liquid until cured. Treat only during the day, taking your regular rest at night.

The same straw water will do for 10 or 12 days if kept in a cool place so it will not sour.

Should it be all over your body, than make enough straw liquid so you can lie under same in a bath tub, keeping head out of this liquid. Do not let straw liquid in your eyes.

Take a copy from this paper for yourself and return mine as I require it for another sick person.

Remember I will not answer any sick person unless an addressed and stamped envelope is sent for a return copy.

Rt. Rev. F.C. Ryan D.P.

Newcastle R.R. no-1 (Extra),

Northumberland County, N.B.

Monsignor Ryan's Model Ship

Besides being known for his folk cures, Monsignor Ryan was also known for helping to preserve a model of a three masted square rigged ship which was on display at the legislative building in Fredericton, N.B., and now is at the N.B. Museum in Saint John.

The model ship was built by Robert Murphy, a draughtsman from Moncton, N.B.. Murphy began his model about 1872 and then moved to Kouchibouguac in 1883 and completed it there in 1890.

When Murphy began his model, he was determined to build it exactly as an actual ship would be built. He very patiently worked every detail down to scale. The model ship's mountings were made from solid brass which Murphy himself cut from solid blocks of metal using tools he had constructed.

Every plank in the hull was steamed and bent into place according to scale. The ship's pumps, capstan, windlass, anchors, winches, davits and chains were all done by hand according to the supposed tonnage of the ship. The final product was a perfect replica of an actual square masted rigger.

When Robert Murphy went to work in New York in 1897, he took along his model ship. For ten years it was displayed at a New York waterfront bar with a placard which offered the ship to anyone who could find a flaw in its design.

During the next ten years there were many who examined the ship's every detail, but when Murphy returned home in 1907, his ship came with him.

Murphy then visited his son-in-law John J. Ryan in Whitneyville, Maine, U.S.A. where he soon met Monsignor Ryan who eventually bought the ship from him.

Murphy later delivered the ship to Monsignor Ryan in Andover, N.B. where Ryan was stationed. From there, Ryan brought the ship to Red Bank, Miramichi where it remained until 1968 when it was loaned to the provincial legislature. Murphy himself lived with Monsignor Ryan for two years until his death in 1914.

Museums in the U.S. and elsewhere were interested in purchasing the model ship, but Monsignor would not sell it. He eventually gave in to John B. McNair's government of the province of New Brunswick in May of 1948, agreeing to allow the ship to be placed on display in a glass case in the N.B. Legislature.

Monsignor Ryan allowed the government to display the ship providing they would restore it to perfect order. He charged them five dollars a year holding fee and agreed after five years that he would be free to sell it as long as he provided a month's notice.

In November of 1950, Mr. Albert Carty was employed to carry out the necessary work to bring the ship back to its original standard of excellence.

Monsignor Ryan was determined to see that the ship did not leave the province of N.B. and put a price of $50,000 for "labour alone" not counting its value as art, and offered it for sale to the province.

The province did not agree to buy the ship, and eventually, Monsignor decided in August, 1968 to loan the ship to the N.B. Museum in Saint John "where it would add immensely to the marine attraction".

Monsignor Ryan was so determined that this piece of art be preserved for the people of New Brunswick that he eventually gave it to the Province as follows:

"I hereby give and bequeath to the Province of New Brunswick, with ownership vested in the New Brunswick Museum, my unnamed plank on frame square rigged ship model built by Robert Murphy, a naval draftsman of Moncton. In so doing I understand and agree that it may be retained and used in such a manner as, at the discretion of the Museum, may be in the best interest of the public... Monsignor F. C. Ryan."

Besides being a folk healer, Monsignor Ryan was instrumental in saving an artistic piece of N.B. history so that future generations could appreciate the era of sail which had been so much a part of our heritage.

Miracle or Just Lucky

Father A. A. McKinnon was a well known priest in the Miramichi area. He carried a stick or shillelagh that was known as "The Black Thorn" and wherever he went, he was in control.

When he was a priest in Miscou, he was told that there was a man who came to church to cause trouble. The first day in the parish, Father McKinnon met him at the gate and told him he was the new priest there and that the man had better realize that there was to be no more trouble or he would have to deal with him personally. That was the end of the trouble.

When he was in Blackville, he would patrol the isles during the annual St. Patrick's Concert held in the church hall. Normally a raucous atmosphere prevailed, but when Father McKinnon walked around with his "Black Thorn" there was perfect silence.

Father McKinnon considered dancing sinful and pointedly let his Blackville congregation know. At one service he is supposed to have said that he knew that some of his parishioners were attending dances in Sunny Corner. He told the young girls that if he caught any of them going there he would make them stand in the back of the church with a horse collar around their necks. As well as being a stern disciplinarian Father McKinnon was not afraid to speak his mind.

He would walk the community after dark with a flashlight and pity help any young girls he found out after dark. My Aunt Delphine (Underhill) Harris told me of Father McKinnon confronting her and her sister one night at the Blackville train station.

"We were there to meet our aunt who was arriving on the train when the flashlight came on and he wanted to know what we were doing there. We told him and he waited until the train arrived and our aunt got off before he left," said Harris.

During mass one Sunday the organist happened to knock over a kneeling bench during a quiet time in the ceremony. Father

McKinnon promptly declared throughout the church "That's right, Susie, knock'er down and we'll build her up tomorrow".

Another time a man from the parish brought in a cord of wood for the church. Father McKinnon looked at it and said "well, you may call it a cord, but it looks like a half a cord to me".

My cousin Carl Burns told me a very interesting story about Father McKinnon the day that there was a fire next door. This was during the 1940's.

Burns said that the Richardson house next door to his parents (Janet and Morrissy Burns) on Digby St. (The back road) in Blackville had caught fire. It was only about twenty feet from their house and the wind was blowing large cinders toward them.

"My father began to move the furniture out of the house in case of fire. Father McKinnon arrived and asked what my father was doing. Father replied the obvious about trying to save some of the furniture. Father McKinnon promptly told him to bring the furniture back in. He then nailed a crucifix to the side of our house and said, `This house will not burn. Don't remove anything'".

Burns added that Father McKinnon did not wait around to see what would develop.

"After he made his declaration, he simply walked away. In his mind nothing was going to happen and nothing did. Was it a miracle or just good luck?"

Elizabeth (Lynch) Underhill: Midwife and Healer

Elizabeth Isadore (Lynch) Underhill was my grandmother. She died when I was very young. I came to know her through a few scattered memories and mostly from stories that I heard of her.

She was born of Irish decent in Craigville, back of Nelson-Miramichi and married my grandfather Alfred John Underhill. She was a diminutive woman of about five foot two, but one who ruled the roost.

Folklore

I am told that she was the unofficial mid-wife of Blackville. She is reported to have always said in any situation "If I can do any good, I'll go". It did not matter the time of day or night.

But it is the many other stories, probably from her Irish background, that make her seem even more special. She was attributed to have a keen sense of being able to cure many ailments.

I was told that when I was very young, I was subject to frequent nose-bleeds. My grandmother would put a metal bottle opener on my back to stop the bleeding.

When I had a fever, she would wrap my feet with Mullein leaves to relieve it, she would put goose grease on my chest for croop, and when I had a sore throat she would wrap my neck with salt herring. I don't know if these cured my illnesses, but they ensured that no one else came close enough to catch them.

She was also supposed to have some special power to stop bleeding. I remember my aunt Effie Burns telling me of calling her mother about her husband Leo who had cut himself. Grandmother told her to go back to him that the bleeding had stopped, and when she did, it had.

It was said that she had "curing hands". She would place her hands on the sick person and apparently, it seemed to work for she was frequently called to numerous incidents through the village and asked to help stop the pain others were experiencing.

My cousin told me of such an incident when he suffered from appendicitis. My grandmother came and placed her hands on his stomach, and he was cured.

Ironically, she herself died in severe pain. The power she had did not work for her.

I have heard that whatever knowledge or power she had, was passed down from generation to generation from a man to a woman to a man. Whether this is true or not, I do not know, but a good number of people in her family and her community certainly believed that she was special and called her in emergencies.

Folklore

Kelly's Bear Stories

Working in the woods has always put men in close contact with nature's animals, and one which most would rather not meet is a bear. Most times a bear will avoid contact with humans, but there are always those few times when a bear does not act in the normal way. That's when trouble begins. Allan Kelly experienced a few of those occasions.

Working in the woods all of his life, it is not surprising that Kelly had encountered some bears and naturally had some "bear stories". He describes one:

"We were five guys peeling pulp during the summer for Frasers. We had built a little camp and had an old coat for the door to keep the flies out. We had molasses and food in the camp, and we had a lot of those old fashioned dippers for drinking from the spring, and we had them hung along the wall. We also had a rifle."

"Through the night, a bear came into the camp looking for the molasses. The guys were frightened because he weighed about 500 pounds. They wanted Joe to shoot him, but he wouldn't. He said that if he missed, the bear would get us. One of the guys started shaking the dippers hanging on the wall and they frightened the bear and he left," said Kelly.

"Another time we were in a camp in Beaverbrook with my brother-in-law Stanley Murray and through the night a bear tried to get into the camp. He took one of those long poles with birch bark on the end for starting fires and chased him into the woods, but I was always afraid to be in the camp by myself," said Kelly.

Looking for molasses!

The Mad Trapper's Miramichi Connection

Perhaps one of the greatest man hunts in Canadian history took place in late 1931 and early 1932. The case was that of Albert Johnson known as "The Mad Trapper" of Rat River in the Northwest Territories and Yukon. The RCMP chased Johnson for over a month through chilling Arctic temperatures until they finally killed him in a shootout on February 17, 1932 on the ice of Eagle River in the Yukon.

Johnson had shot and wounded an RCMP officer who had approached his cabin to inquire about his activities. He was given the name "The Mad Trapper" by the media, but in actual fact Johnson was an excellent trapper who was prepared to survive in the -40 degrees Fahrenheit of the Arctic. The fact that he crossed the Richardson Mountains in the Yukon in mid winter was considered a feat in itself.

The Miramichi has in its own small way a piece of that history.

Eugene Gillis of Red Bank was an RCMP officer at that time serving in the Peace River area of Northern Alberta. Gillis knew some of the key people involved in the actual man hunt, but it is more than memories that he has brought with him.

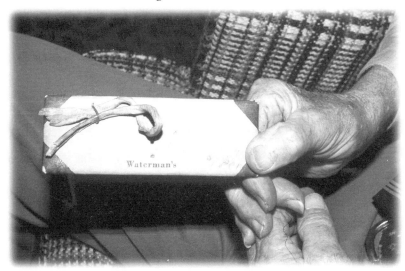

A piece of lacing from The Mad Trappers Snowshoes.

Gillis actually snipped a piece of lacing from Albert Johnson's snowshoes and has kept it as a momento of the famed hunt. The snowshoes are preserved in the RCMP Museum in Regina, Saskatchewan.

"The snowshoes were odd. They were different than most we see. They did not have the long piece of wood hanging out from the back. His had a rounded end to them," said Gillis.

Gillis kept a scrapbook of many events surrounding his RCMP career. Several pages have newspaper clippings of the Albert Johnson affair.

There is a sketched photograph of Johnson with its caption which reads "Albert Johnson, mystery man of Rat River and object of the wildest manhunt in the annuals of the Mounted".

Another clipped photograph is of a sketch depicting RCMP officer Alfred King who was shot by Johnson as he approached his fortified cabin.

The caption on the photograph reads, "Without warning Johnson fired through the door. King Tottered".

On the photograph it is noted that Gillis had written, "I knew Cpl. King".

Gillis also said that he had met Edgar Millen who was also wounded by Johnson.

"I travelled with Millen on a train once and was told a lot about the whole event," said Gillis.

Gillis reminisced about stories he had heard of how Johnson's cabin was actually partially underground and built almost like a fortress.

He told stories of how Johnson slipped away in the night undetected by RCMP officers after they had confronted him in his cabin, how he was tracked, how he actually put his snowshoes on backwards to deceive his trackers, and how World War I ace W. R. "Wop" May was called in from Edmonton to use his plane to track Johnson. It was the first time a plane was used in a manhunt.

"Wop May's plane was equipped with skis so he could land almost anywhere."

Johnson was heading over the Richardson Mountains into the Yukon hoping to make his way across the border to Alaska, U.S.A. where he figured he could escape. He had travelled within a herd of migrating caribou so that his tracks would be obliterated by the hooves of the herd.

With the help of Wop May, officers finally cornered Johnson on the bend of Eagle River for a final shoot out. There were shots exchanged and Albert Johnson was captured by the RCMP.

Gillis who turned 90 the Thanksgiving weekend 1998, was

Eugene Gillis

amazed at how many RCMP officers would talk to him and say "I hear you have a piece of Albert Johnson's snow shoes".

Gillis smiled as he held up the snipped raw-hide lacing which is attached to a piece of leather approximately three by eight inches with the brand name "Waterman's". Printed roughly in pen beside the lacing is "A. Johnson Mad Trapper".

Cougars in New Brunswick?

There has been a long running debate over the existence of cougars in New Brunswick. For years the official line has been "no cougars", but many a woodsman and others have reported sightings.

In the mid 1990's, a sample of "scat" was confirmed as being from a cougar. But Ralph Thompson did not need that evidence to convince him of the presence of a cougar in the province.

Thompson is not your average person in terms of being

around the woods and being familiar with animals and their ways. He has long been an outdoorsman and had the unique hobby of "hunting bobcats." Thus he would be a reliable person to be making an observation about cougars.

Thompson said that he used to shoot up to three bobcats a day, but now only uses the more humane approach of capturing his prey with a camera. He still has hounds, and over the years he has come to know a lot about "cats" in general.

"I got to know a lot about them, what they ate and where they were most likely to be and the sounds they would make when they were in mating season, when hungry and when they were angry."

Thompson even won a "world treeing contest" in Nova Scotia where hunters from across North America participated in treeing bobcats.

Once Thompson even played with a bobcat which he had treed.

"My dogs and I had treed a cat, so I decided to climb up toward him. I got to about five feet from him. I had a stick with me, and began to push it behind his ear in a scratching fashion. He didn't move. He wanted me to continue because he actually liked it," said Thompson.

His many years of experience with cats make Thompson a reliable source among those who claim to have spotted a cougar. His encounter took place just above Nelson Hollow near Doaktown, N.B..

"I was managing some camps near Nelson Hollow. I was originally from P.E.I. and had come over here to work. It was about 11:00 p.m. at night, and a really dark night in August. You literally could not see your hand in front of you," said Thompson.

"We had a little Boston Bulldog and I decided to take a walk from the camp to the road which was about 300 to 400 yards away. I reached the highway and then started back. It was very silent. That's when I heard footsteps behind me. I thought it was one of the boys from the camp. I stopped and the footsteps stopped too. They sounded to be about 30 yards behind me. I started and the footsteps started, and I stopped again and they stopped too. I wondered why they had stopped when I did, because it was dark and no one could see me."

Thompson reported that this mysterious behaviour continued until he was finally back at the camp.

"My little dog was terrified. He kept trying to jump up into my arms. When we were about five or six yards from the camp, whatever was following me went into the ditch. Then I knew it was an animal. I started making noises and pretended to bark at it as if I was a dog. Then it let out this scream. It started like a low growl and ended up in a scream. I'm sure you could have heard it in Doaktown. It did this three or four times. I got tired playing with it and finally went into the camp."

Thompson said that the next morning he looked in the ditch where he thought the animal had been. It had broken off good sized alders where it had been walking around.

A few days later he mentioned it to the wardens who said that it had probably been a bobcat that was after his dog.

"I accepted that explanation because I was new here and had never heard a bobcat, but after hunting bobcats for years and knowing what I do about them and their sounds, I know that this was not a bobcat, and that you would never hear a bobcat walking behind you. The biggest bobcat might weigh 30 pounds tops, and they are like a house cat, pretty quiet when they move," said Thompson.

It was long after the event that Thompson actually knew that it was a cougar that had been following him and screaming at him.

"It was years later that I finally knew what had been following me. I was watching a TV program dealing with two cougars, and one of them let out a scream. As soon as I heard it, I knew what it was. Once you hear a scream like that you never forget it. It was a cougar."

In all the hunting he had done, Thompson had never seen a cougar track until the late winter of 1977.

"It was at the top of the Cains River Road near the power line about the first week of April. I was starting in when I saw a set of tracks and decided to trail them to a thicket. I couldn't make the track out as clearly as I would have liked on the road because the snow was drifting a bit, but near the thicket I could see that it was just a bit smaller than my hand."

The track was deeper than most he'd seen. He estimated that it was made by an animal weighing about 100 pounds based on how deep it had sunk into the snow.

"Then I found what I was looking for. It was a mark about three inches long where its tail had hit the snow in the middle of the tracks as the tracks went deeper. It was a cougar track. So, based upon those two experiences, I'm positive there are at least a few cougars around the Miramichi," said Thompson.

The Red Bank Cannon Ball

One of the more interesting transportation links in the Miramichi during the late 1920's was what came to be known as "The Red Bank Cannon Ball".

The Red Bank Cannon Ball was a bus that was operated by business entrepreneur Stanford McKibbon of Red Bank and ran from Red Bank and surrounding communities such as Sillikers, Cassilis, Sunny Corner and points on the way to its destination of Newcastle.

In 1928, Stanford took over the bus franchise from John Ferguson of Newcastle. With the assistance of John Porter of Sunny Corner, Stanford began building his own buses. To build his first bus, he bought a new Ford truck and used the truck chassis as the base on which to place a sturdy frame structure covered with sheet metal. The buses travelled to Newcastle twice daily from Red Bank and the surrounding areas.

Since most people in those days did not have cars, they were very happy to have Stanford's bus line as a means of travel. While the rough, bumpy, unpaved roads meant much discomfort for the passengers, they enjoyed the opportunity to socialize with some good conversation mixed on occasion with a little gossip.

The Red Bank Cannon Ball buses.

When people arrived in Red Bank by the noon bus, they were often invited by Stanford and Emeline to come over to the house for dinner. As well, all of the employees including the bus drivers, store clerks, and sometimes even the lumbermen ate their meals with the McKibbon family.

As the demand grew, there was an additional bus run added for late Saturday night. This "midnight run" was an important service, but from time to time it also created a few minor rules-related problems for the driver if someone may have had a drop or two too many.

Stanford kept several buses in operation and the children can remember painting them in the spring. On one occasion young Barbara made an unusual mixture of paints which resulted in a bus getting a coat of paint in a bright pea green. It quickly received the nickname "The Green Hornet" after a popular radio program of that time.

The Green Hornet was used exclusively for freight pickup at the train station and for deliveries of groceries and farm supplies to customers in the community. As Stanford often ordered his supplies by the boxcar, a truck, or in his case a bus, was required for efficient delivery.

The bus served the community in a variety of ways. Not only was it a means of passenger transportation, but also was a means of mail and parcel delivery. The bus driver would drop off parcels or letters to people on the way to Newcastle.

It was not unusual to pick up and drop off groceries purchased in town or at McKibbon's General Store, deliver sacks of feed or flour, and even pick up a pint of spirits for the odd fellow.

The cost of a return trip to Newcastle was 25 cents, with one way being 15 cents. But it was more than just what the bus did, that really gave it its character, and character it had.

The bus took its name as an off shoot of two songs that were well known at the time, "The Wabash Cannon Ball" and Wilf Carter's "Rattlin' Cannon Ball". It spawned a local ballad about the bus which came to be known as "The Red Bank Cannon Ball" and consequently gave the bus its lore.

McKibbon operated a regular bus and also had what was known as "the overflow bus" which was also part of the story surrounding the Red Bank Cannon Ball.

McKibbon and his drivers, including Norman Mather, Phil LeBlanc, Leo McKibbon, Harry Young, Chester Bryenton and Charlie Wilson would ferry their passengers to Newcastle, particularly on weekends, where they would go about their business and return home on the bus when the stores closed at 10 p.m. Friday nights.

After the bus made its trip home to Red Bank, the overflow bus would return to Newcastle to pick up those who had stayed to watch the Saturday night movie or "show" as it was known locally, and those who had stayed to play some pool.

The "Overflow" would leave Newcastle at 1:00 a.m. or close to it, depending on whom the passengers told the driver he had to wait for. It was an important part of the philosophy that everyone should be able to get home, and often schedules were thus set. Seldom was anyone left without a drive home.

The trip home was more than just transportation. There would be an abundance of stories told, songs sung, courting done and most probably the odd drop of spirits consumed. It often became a form of mobile entertainment almost as important as the stationary entertainment in town.

If a person did not have the money for the return trip he was certainly not left behind.

When the bus became crowded, a few of the young fellows would be asked to get in the huge trunk at the back with the door left ajar. Someone whimsically noted that it was a wonder they were not gassed, but everyone survived and had fun.

The seats were along the sides and were made from dyed feed sacks and filled with straw as cushions. As winter travel required heat, Stanford installed a wood stove inside each of his buses. These were tended and stoked, as required, by the passengers themselves.

One former passenger said "You could see her pullin' out of Newcastle with two feet of flame coming out the smoke stack of the old stove".

The road to Newcastle was pretty rough in places and the Cannon Ball could be heard rattling along for quite the distance. One night it got stuck in a mud hole in Whitney and spent the night there. Here was a song often sung while aboard the Red Bank Cannon Ball.

The Red Bank Cannon Ball
(Sung to the tune of The Wabash Cannon Ball)

Come gather round me, comrades
And listen while I tell
About the good old ramblin' days
You have heard someone tell

First I saw the driver
Then heard old Stanford call
"All aboard, we're off, boys
On the Red Bank Cannon Ball"

Folklore

She always blew the whistle
On Allen Tozer's hill
They knew the danger signal
By the whistle oh so shrill !

Sou'westers liked to ride her
You often heard them call
We're headed for Newcastle
On the Red Bank Cannon Ball

She travelled down to Boom Road
Where no one is allowed
And when they reach Strathadam
They pick up all the crowd

The rich men ride the front seats
In all their splendours grand
The poor ones ride the back seats
A girl on every hand

Then down at Curtis' Corner
We'd pick up old Joe Wall
We're headed for Newcastle
On the Red Bank Cannon Ball

Laura made her mind up
One day she'd go to town
When she stepped on the Cannon Ball
The seats they sure went down

The Cannon Ball rolls by, boys
I think I'll let her go
I see another coming
I'll catch the "Overflow"

"All aboard, we're off, boys"
You can hear old Stanford call
"We're headed for Newcastle
On the Red Bank Cannon Ball"

(Repeat the last stanza)

Miramichi Folksong Festival: A Living Museum

The Miramichi Folksong Festival is an icon of Miramichi culture. The first Festival was held in the Beaverbrook Theatre and Town Hall in Newcastle September 3rd to 5th in 1958 with CBC's Ken Homer acting as Master of Ceremonies.

First organized by Louise Manny, the festival enters its 42nd consecutive year in August , 1999. The festival is a living museum of Miramichi history and culture.

The whole idea of collecting and then presenting Miramichi folksongs in festival form began with one of Miramichi's most famous sons, Lord Beaverbrook.

As a boy Beaverbrook loved to listen to and sing the old songs of the Miramichi with "The Jones Boys" being one of his favourites. Louise Manny recalled that Beaverbrook approached her in 1947 and said:

"Why don't you go out and collect New Brunswick folksongs? I'll send you a fine recording machine."

Beaverbrook even used "The Jones Boys" to break the ice in major conferences immediately following World War II. At the Yalta Conference Beaverbrook was reported to have taught it to Stalin.

When Beaverbrook donated a set of chimes to the University of New Brunswick in Fredericton in 1940, he arranged for them to play the tune of "The Jones Boys".

With the help of Bessie Crocker, Manny began their collection. Little did they realize the wealth of material they would find, or the response their efforts would have.

Once word got out that they were collecting, and that Lord Beaverbrook was interested in them, the songs came pouring in. An article by Ian Sclanders in "Mayfair" December 1953 states:

"And everybody seemed eager to help. Wherever [Manny] went people volunteered information about singers. A lot of singers themselves, so bent with years they could hardly walk, travelled to Newcastle to offer their songs. They were motivated by sentiment, not vanity. They wanted their beloved songs to be preserved."

Mary Duthie in a paper titled "The Miramichi Folksong Festival" records:

"One elderly woodsman sang a full one hundred of them himself before he paused and shook his head sadly and said he was sorry he couldn't be more help but his memory was failing a bit lately."

Manny in the course of her research collected over 400 songs, some in English, some French and even some in Micmac. In 1968 Manny and James Wilson compiled the first printed collection of Miramichi songs titled *Songs of Miramichi*.

In 1948 Manny began a weekly radio program on the local station CKMR with purpose of encouraging more singers to come forth with their songs. The program aired every Wednesday afternoon at 2:00 p.m.. This got Manny into a fair bit of trouble with the lumber companies of the day as their workers would steal away from their work to listen to the songs. After many protests, Manny did move the program to Sunday to keep everyone happy.

Miramichiers will remember local broadcaster and singer Art Matchett

Memorial to Dr. Louise Manny.

as he would often sing impromptu songs over the air much to the delight of all.

It was this love of their own music and tradition that inspired the actual festival. Manny gathered many singers and their friends for a "get together festival" feeling it would "provide entertainment for our own visitors to the province, and it will also help to keep alive and flourishing the folk songs of the Miramichi which [are] part and parcel of our history and culture".

Manny continued her efforts with the festival for twelve years when failing health forced her to step aside as director. The role then fell into the capable hands of Maizie Mitchell who added "arabic songs" she had learned in the Magdalen Islands. During her years at the helm Mitchell placed her own touch to the festival closing each night's performance with her beautiful rendition of "Bon Soir, mes amis, bon soir".

Mitchell expressed some concern about the future of the festival. They were not getting a lot of younger singers coming along, and she feared the festival would die with the performers who were themselves on the decline.

Duthie reports that "the singers were getting too old" and "too sick to perform" and young performers felt "out of place and unwelcome." Traditionally, performers sang their selections without any musical accompaniment, and younger performers were uncomfortable without their instruments.

One story even had world renowned folksinger Pete Seeger requesting to perform at the festival, but Dr. Manny turned him down because she would not allow instruments, and did not want professionals who might discourage the local performers.

Mitchell continued in her role until 1983 when she requested that Susan Butler take over. Under the directorship of Butler and the folksong committee, the festival has not only survived, but has grown and has brought younger and newer talent into the fore while still preserving the spirit, songs and tradition of the earlier festivals.

The earlier songs were known in many cases as "come-all ye's" as that was often the opening line which requested the listeners attention. Wayne Curtis in his article for *The Atlantic Advocate* in February 1985 wrote: "It was said that, the Miramichier had a song for just about everything he did, from working at the sawmill, to milking a cow or picking blueberries."

Duthie records, "The lumbermen, shipbuilders, fishermen and farmers who lived [here] worked hard, but they often sang as they worked or to entertain themselves when work was done. They would sing as they walked to town, drove to work, or as they waited at their nets. They sang when they milked the cows, cut the wood, scrubbed the floors or built buildings. Often the song chosen fitted the task or the time it took. Milking songs were the rhythm that matched the chore thereby soothing the cows and making the job more enjoyable. Similarly, a song sung while cutting wood would match the rhythm of the cross-cut saw".

Some of these songs could last up to 20 minutes or more and certainly required a lot from the performer not only in stamina, but also in memory. It would not be unusual to hear a performer stop on stage and regroup, often with the help from someone from the audience who were very much a part of each performance.

I remember a particular performance when writer and actor Peter Pacey was presenting his skit titled "Bull of the Woods" whereby his character had to portray the toughness of the lumberjack. When Pacey recited his lines to the effect that he was the toughest man around, someone in the audience shouted out, and meant it, "Oh, step outside and we'll see".

Many of the songs were also brought over from Europe and preserved the past culture of many who came here. The topics of many of the earlier songs were often tragic dealing with shipwrecks, disasters and lost loves, or the dangers of busting a log jam with the often fatal results as recorded in the famous "Jam on Gerry's Rock".

One of the earliest Miramichi songs sung was "Mullins Boom" named after the County jailer Mullin. It was composed and sung by the prisoners in the county jail. Other Miramichi songs which stand out include John Calhoun's Peter Emberley, Larry Gorman's "The Scow on Cowden Shore", John Jardine's "The Miramichi Fire", Martin Sullivan's "The Bluebird", Michael Whalen's "The Dungarvon Whooper", Paul Kingston's "The Wayerton Driver", Davey Hunter and Charles Kiscadden's "Duffy's Hotel", William McKay's "Peelhead" and of course James Barry's "The Jones Boys".

The singing of the songs was a complicated affair, not so much in actual musical ability, but in the strict traditions that had to be observed. Audiences were not so much concerned with how good the performer's voice was or even if he could carry a tune. It was the story that was important.

Sclanders writes "a singer with too much rhythm, too many vocal inflections, is frowned on as a show-off, and a singer who sings the last line of his song, instead of dropping his voice and speaking it, is automatically branded as a raw amateur- and not a very promising one either".

Often after saying the last line performers would end with a "whoop" to indicate that the song was finished and then added a little jig or step dance as he left the stage.

There were also the taboos about who would sing what songs as certain songs became part of the personality of individual singers, and for someone to sing a song normally sung by a specific performer amounted to "fighting words".

There were also the traditions of who would open and close the festival, a role often reserved for the late Wilmot MacDonald. Anyone violating the regular order was quickly taken to task.

One year when I was giving the introductory remarks on opening night, I paid tribute to the late Nick Underhill who had passed away. I "attempted" two lines from his "Jones Boys" when Wilmot came to life at the back of the theatre commenting to an observer something to the effect "What was that young whipper-snapper doing up there as I am the one who opens the festival" until he realized that I was not really doing the opening song.

Over the years there have been certain people who have been the backbone and foundation of the festival including Stanley and Wilmot MacDonald. Wilmot was even recorded by the Smithsonian Institute. When asked to come to Washington to be recorded, he is said to have replied, "If you want my songs then you'll have to come here and get them." No festival was complete without Wilmot's singing of "The Lumberman's Alphabet".

There were Sammy Jagoe, Frank and Ray Estey, Jared MacLean, Perley and Marie Hare, Nick Underhill, Paul Kingston, and of course Allan Kelly who has performed at all 41 festivals to date.

Later performers include Susan Butler and daughters Shannon and Kathleen, Mary Butler, John McKay, Robert McKay, Kevin Driscoll, Charlie Russell, John Lordon, Hubert Sweezey, George Fulton, the Aubey family of Percy, and sons Johnny, Armand, and Paul, Anthony Ward, Norman Young, Andy McGraw, Gary Silliker, Tom Gregan, Roger Lanteigne, Reg Lynch, fiddlers Matilda Murdock, Clarence Lynch and Jim Morrison, Vera Campbell, Charlie Slane, Steve Heckbert, Harold R. P. Whitney, Velma Kelly, Sandy Hogan, Mrs. Allan MacDonald, Seraphie Martin, Captain Glen Lealand, Derwin Gowan, Rev. Wilfred Langmaid, Alexander Baisley, Robert Thomas, Bill LeBlanc, Frankie McKibbon, Cathy and Peter Daigle and daughter Jennifer, Melanie Ross, The Gillis Family, The Miramichi Fiddlers, Bannon and Joanne Morrisey, Nelson Doyle Dancers, Landry School of Dance, Brandie Mills, and Shayla Steeves to name a few.

No festival would be complete without mention of step dancer Francis Taylor whose dancing and gyrations immediately bring the audience alive. Not a performance goes by without at least someone from the audience hollering, "Driver Francis", a phrase that has become very much a Miramichi expression for anyone who goes at anything with gusto.

As an organizer, Butler has been very successful at walking a tight line between the traditional singers and new talent.

Festival organizer and performer Susan Butler.

"People hate change, but we have gradually brought a younger generation into the performing circle, and we have brought some professionals into the fore as well. They all share the same stage without any ill feelings. As a matter of fact they seem to compliment each other. As I have always said, the locals are the cake and the professionals are the icing, but you can't have the icing without the cake," said Butler.

Butler has also extended the reach of the festival from just three nights.

"We now have 14 shows in a five day stretch and this year we will be having a multi-cultural night. We promote our culture about eight months of the year with something going on or by being in the planning stage at all times. We have also added workshops with each festival where the professionals work with new and younger performers. They all enjoy the camaraderie," said Butler.

The festival has also hosted the 16th Annual N.B. Country Hall of Fame Awards.

Butler has shared the Miramichi stage with such notable performers as Valdy, Rita McNeil, The Barra MacNeils, Men of the Deep, Ashley McIssac, John Allen Cameron, Stompin' Tom Connors, The Rankin Family, Graham and Eleanor Townsend, Frank Patterson, Mary O'Hara, Clary Croft, Rollins Cross, Tips Splinter, Tom Lewis, Evans and Doherty, Connie and Paul, Wakamiwailers, Dave Mallett, John Gracie, Tanglefoot, Cindy Botineau, Steve Foote, Theresa Doyle, The Kidd Brothers, Gallagher & Galbraith, Gordon Stobbe, Garnet Rogers, Tess LeBlanc,

Cindy Thompson Butineau, Eddie Poirier, Aubrey Hanson, Ivan and Vivian Hicks, Ned Landry, Dan McKinnon, Tom Leadbeater, Stacy Reed, Pete Doiron, David Stone, Paul and Lutia Lauzon and Bill Staines.

The festival has been opened by such famous people as David Adams Richards, Marshall Button, Premier Frank McKenna, Senator Margaret Anderson, Wayne Curtis, Herb Curtis, Senator Burchill, Lieutenant-Governor George Stanley, Harvey Kirk and Glen Misner.

Noted folklorists who have attended the festival are University of Maine's Sandy Ives, Helen Creighton of N.S., Charlotte Cormier from Moncton, and Margaret Steiner from Indiana who will be attending her fourteenth festival this year.

Over the years, there has been a tradition of visiting the "Black Horse Tavern" across the street by performers and patrons of the festival alike. Perley Hare returned from such a visit to sing his song and then soon after passed away. One can only assume that he died happy. Now the festival has even spawned its own jam sessions at the Black Horse. When the regular performances finish, many move to the Black Horse where a spontaneous festival of its own begins with singers and performers going on long into the night. As a result of the love of folksong of his river, Beaverbrook has helped preserve a very integral part of Miramichi culture. There have been numerous recordings of the songs, most notably the Beaverbrook Collection, several recordings of the original festival performers, and several records put out by individual performers such as Marie Hare, Allan Kelly and Charlie Slane as well as recording tapes and CD's by many of the more recent singers such as Susan Butler, Stephen Heckbert and others.

All in all, the future of the Miramichi Folksong Festival looks healthy in the very capable hands of Susan Butler.

If we watch carefully and listen closely, we may even witness the ghost of Lord Beaverbrook driving to pick up Edmond Robichaud to sing the old songs for him in his car, as he did in the late 1940's. Thanks, in part, to Lord Beaverbrook, those songs continue to be sung today.

Radio Street and The Wireless Field

Radio Street in the former Town of Newcastle and now part of the City of Miramichi West has an interesting history which eventually gave the street its present name.

Adjacent to the top of Radio Street just below the CN Railway Line was what was once known as "The Wireless Field". The Wireless Field encompassed the area roughly enclosed today by Radio Street on the east, to the King George Highway on the south, Edward Street on the west and Roger Street on the north. It housed what was known as the Newcastle Wireless Station which was owned by Universal Radio Syndicate Ltd. whose head office was located in London, England.

The area, which comprised approximately 54 acres, was originally the properties of James Falconer, Edward Hickey, Edward Woodworth and A. J. Morrison. These were purchased by Universal Radio Syndicate for the purpose of establishing a wireless station that was to be part of a string of similar stations intended to circle the world as one huge communication system.

Another station similar to this was built at Ballybunion, Ireland, and the pair were the two most powerful in the world.

The company had purchased patents for control of the Poulsen Wireless System which was similar to that used by the Marconi Wireless System, and intended to operate a commercial wireless service.

Valdemar Poulsen was born in Denmark November 23, 1869. He was an inventor working with the Copenhagen Telephone Company. He invented the forerunner of the tape recorder known as a "telegraphone", but it did not gain much acceptance in its day. He continued his work with radio signals and in 1903 obtained an English patent for his work where in he developed an arc system that could run at 1,000 khz a second which is about the middle of the present day radio broadcast band.

Poulsen himself, along with several Danes, Swedes and Germans, came to Newcastle to oversee the actual commissioning of the station. Poulsen achieved recognition for his work, but following World War I his system became obsolete with new technology replacing it.

However, the wireless station did play an important part in the history of Newcastle and in the Canadian War effort.

Newcastle was chosen as the site for the station and was considered the main site on the Atlantic coast with its messages being forwarded by the Great North Western Telegraph Co.

Newcastle engineer William E. Fish was hired to tour New Brunswick to find a suitable location between Campbellton and Moncton. He convinced the company's chief engineer, Sir (Dr.) Erskine Murray, to select Newcastle because there were no obstructions that would retard the sending and receiving of messages between Newcastle and the Atlantic Ocean.

Construction of the site began in 1913. There was one large steel tower 500 feet high that was built in England, shipped here in sections and then assembled.

The company hired several natives from a Mohawk-Iroquois tribe from Quebec to assemble the towers as they were considered experts at working at such heights.

There were also six wooden towers between 100 to 200 feet high built on the property as well as a generating station and transmitting facility. When finished, the station was capable of transmitting 80 words a minute and employed around 50 men.

Anna Allen in a paper titled "The Wireless Station" records "The people of Newcastle said that they looked like a giant hand of seven fingers pointing to the sky".

The generating station housed two large Diesel engines with 225 horsepower each. Each engine weighed 30 tons. It was said one of these could have supplied the whole town of Newcastle with power.

The facility was completed in 1914 with Mr. John Colton of Montreal as chief censor and operator while D. A. Jackson of Chatham, N.B. was chief engineer. Another engineer who played a large part in the station was Swede Charles Lund who probably worked there longer than anybody, being asked to stay on as caretaker.

But as the station opened, World War I was also under way, and naturally, a communications system such as the one in Newcastle was considered of paramount importance.

Alex LeRoy, who researched the Station in Newcastle wrote:

"The war came, and 200 soldiers marched up with bayonets bristling and the station was commandeered for the Admiralty and placed under heavy guard. Barracks were built there. Day and night through the war years operators sat at their key boards and controls of what was probably one of the most important stations in the Service of the British Admiralty."

The messages all came in the form of long columns of numbers as they were all in secret code. Nine copies were then sent to different military centres and Naval bases to be decoded.

If intelligence found out a message from an enemy station was to be passed along, the Newcastle station was informed and operators had to pass long hours waiting to intercept the enemy message, all the while knowing that failure to do so might result in the deaths of hundreds.

Nobody was permitted into the facility without the proper password. LeRoy stated that "Sometimes when they got a new batch of soldiers on duty you had quite a job to get in at all. You had to talk as hard as a Philadelphia Lawyer to get in".

When the station was being built, some who worked on it were German engineers. When war came, they were interned, but escaped probably to the United States or South America. When asked whether the soldiers searched for them, Charles Lund is reported to have said:

"After they were gone. They were good fellows, good law-abiding citizens just like anybody else. They didn't have anything to do with starting the war. I don't think anybody who knew them was very sorry they got away."

Some people trumped up their involvement saying that the Germans knew what was going on and were part of a conspiracy to build a communications system that would help their war effort.

Some said that the Germans thought Canada would rebel after the war broke out and would side with Germany as would the United States.

Lund recorded the following in regard to this attitude.

"Germany was kind of over optimistic, eh?... But - the same question you have been asking yourself - Why would Germany, the year before the war, build a wireless station for the nation that was almost bound to be her enemy?"

There were 70 soldiers on duty at the site. Along with this Anna Allen states that the sight was "used as a training and recruiting depot through the war years."Pictures of the site show numerous army tents pitched amongst the towers.

When the war ended the Newcastle Wireless Station was eventually sold to the Marconi Wireless Telegraph Company for $25,000. The war had left the Universal Radio Syndicate insolvent, and superior research and technological advances soon made the Poulsen system obsolete before it found any universal application.

The Marconi Company did some experimental work there, but found little use for the facility and permitted it to lie dormant, although they kept renewing their license to operate it for many years. Charles Lund was hired on as care-taker and continued in this role until the station was dismantled.

The station site thus became a ghost of a past era, standing erect against the sky-line, and was used as a pasture for cows. Expensive equipment was left gathering dust. Allen recorded:

"Looking inside you could see switchboards and copper coils, pieces of arc apparatus, receiving sets, storage cells, tens of thousands of dollars of equipment gathering dust and falling to pieces. Looking at it you would think it looked like a workshop of some fictional scientists."

In 1935 the wear and tear of the wind and overall neglect made the towers a safety hazard and they were torn down except for the main tower which was removed in 1950.

Two of the more prominent buildings which were part of the original Wireless Station in Newcastle have been transformed into businesses and act as living monuments to a very interesting part of the history of Miramichi.

In 1949, the main generating station, which had underground tunnels, was sold. For a while Anderson's mill stored spool wood there before Abe Asoyuf bought it and converted it to a brick factory. Eventually it was purchased for a machine shop by Gerard Arseneau who later sold it to William (Bill) Allen who owns it today. It still functions as Castle Machine Works at 142 Roger St.

The other main building of the complex was the one used by the telegraph operators. It was purchased by Frank Morris in the mid 1950's and still exists in the family today as Morris Wholesale Ltd. at 125 Petrie St.

When you drive up Radio Street in Miramichi, you can now appreciate the rich history which gave the street its name.

The former main generating station of the Wireless Field.

Legends

Miramichi Home to
Two Fathers of Confederation

The birth of any country is a memorable event, and the Miramichi can lay claim to a very significant part of the birth of Canada. Of the 36 acknowledged Fathers of Confederation, two were from the Miramichi. In no other part of Canada were there two Fathers of Confederation whose homes were only five miles apart.

Peter Mitchell

The Honourable Peter Mitchell and the Honourable John Mercer Johnson both participated in the early movements which brought union to the British Colonies.

Johnson attended the Quebec, Charlottetown and London conferences while Mitchell was an official participant in the Quebec and London conferences and an unofficial participant in Charlottetown.

Mitchell was born January 24, 1824 in Newcastle. He attended grammar school and went on to study law and set up a practice with John Mercer Johnson of Chatham.

However, Mitchell's real interest lay in lumbering and shipbuilding. He was involved in the construction of 15 ships, and later became president of the Mitchell Steamship Company. His vessels plied the sea lanes between the Maritimes and Montreal in summer and then moved to Portland, Maine in the winter. His shipyard was located just down river from the present Morrissy Bridge where today's wharf is.

Mitchell then became interested in politics and after an unsuccessful bid in the election of 1852, he was elected as a Liberal to the N.B. Legislature in 1856. His fellow Miramichier and law partner, John Mercer Johnson was also elected in the neighbouring district. The two became known as the "Northumberland County Smashers". They championed the cause of Confederation and defeated the government of Charles Fisher.

In the legislature, Mitchell was to become very close to Samuel Leonard Tilley. In 1860 Mitchell was made a member of the Legislative Council from which he was able to push forth his confederate views.

Mitchell not only wanted Confederation, but also a national railway. He worked tirelessly toward bringing the Intercolonial Railway along a northern route which would pass through the Miramichi. Tilley and his allies favoured the southern route which would better accommodate Saint John.

Mitchell maintained that the railroad was necessary to remove the isolation of the Miramichi in the winter when the river was frozen. He also felt that the railroad would increase the lumbering trade and open the area for mineral development. For those who still needed convincing, he played on the fact that the southern route would be too close to the Americans should war break out.

Mitchell heightened people's fears of annexation and taxation by the United States and finally was successful in having the northern route accepted, but not before the confederate party was defeated, including Tilley. Mitchell himself retained his seat and was the last remaining voice for union.

The Lieutenant Governor highly respected Mitchell, and with a push from Britain, Mitchell was able to bring down the government and become the Premier of New Brunswick in 1866.

The fear of the Fenian movement helped Mitchell's causes. This was an Irish group in the United States which wanted independence for Ireland,

and thereby threatened to mount attacks on Canada as a British colony. The Fennians were basically ignored by the U.S. government, but by merely existing, they caused uneasiness along the Canadian border. Mitchell used this threat to his advantage as he was swept to victory and appointed a delegate to go to London to work out the final details of Confederation.

Mitchell served in the Senate from 1867-72. However, Mitchell and the Prime Minister at the time, Sir John A MacDonald, did not always see eye to eye. There were many disagreements between the two. Mitchell was re-elected as Member of Parliament for Northumberland - Miramichi in 1874, defeated in 1878, but re-elected twice more before finally being defeated in 1891.

Mitchell then went on to become Canada's first Minister of Marine and Fisheries. He created an international incident with the Americans over their ships fishing in Canadian waters. Mitchell built a fleet of six naval vessels to enforce Canada's fishing rights, and actually seized several American vessels when they entered Canadian waters. Mitchell was also responsible for the building of lighthouses and navigational aids along Canada's coast.

He was so respected that he actually won a case for the widow Murphy of Barnaby whose cow had been killed by a train. Mitchell demanded retribution from the railway, and mounted a one man attack in Parliament which eventually resulted in the cow being paid for by the railway.

In 1885 Mitchell bought the *Montreal Herald* but took little interest in its editorial policy. He was made Inspector of Fisheries for Quebec, New Brunswick and Nova Scotia in the Laurier government in March, 1897. But after a stroke in the summer of 1899, and a second attack on October 25 of the same year, he was found dead in Montreal's Windsor Hotel where he had lived the latter part of his life.

Mitchell was known as the man who brought the railroad to northern N.B., a timber merchant, shipbuilder and witty orator, but most of all he was honoured as a Father of Confederation.

He was honoured by the former town of Newcastle by having "Mitchell Street" named after him. Mitchell Street is now part of the

City of Miramichi. Mitchell is buried in the graveyard of St. James and St. John United Church (Newcastle) Miramichi.

Some of Mitchell's artifacts are still in the possession of town and city authorities. A candle-like centrepiece(epergne) and gold watch presented to Mitchell in 1874 were the property of the former Town of Newcastle. The gold watch came back to Mitchell's birth place almost by accident. The former Doreen Menzies of Whitney, N. B. (Mrs. Daniel Arbuckle) noticed the watch advertised in an auction in Ottawa and made arrangements to procure it for Newcastle.

The Town of Newcastle also owns Mitchell's cradle which was presented to Lord Beaverbrook. The cradle had been passed down through the Urquhart family.

In 1941 there was a plaque erected in the Newcastle Post Office by the government of Canada. It was later moved to the Town Square where it stands today as one of Canada's "Historic Sites and Monuments".

In 1969 the Mitchell grave in the St. James and St. John United Church Cemetery was remodeled with a granite stone donated by Nelson Monuments of Sussex and installed by Smith Contractors. It has a plaque similar to the one in the Town Square. Ironically, the cemetery is just across the road from where Peter Mitchell's father ran a hotel and tavern at the corner of the King's Highway and Henry Street.

An interesting anecdote is quoted by Brian Casey in his thesis titled "The Political Career of Peter Mitchell". Casey says that the story was told by Miramichi Senator S. P. Burchill. Apparently Mitchell's wife, the former Isabella Carvell, was a widow of James Gough, a Saint John policeman.

She often addressed temperance and bible meetings. One day as she was speaking at such an occasion, she began to read a passage from the "Acts of the Apostles" and began with "And Peter says" when one man in the room jumped up and shouted "Peter says we must have Confederation at all costs".

Famous folk poet Michael Whalen said it best in his poem "Peter Mitchell" when he eulogized him:

> *Ah, he is dead, the grand old man*
> *Beyond the three score years and ten,*
> *Who in the old time led the van,*
> *The foremost mid the foremost then.*
>
> *When in Confederation's cause*
> *He lent heroic helping hand*
> *To formulate the liberal laws*
> *That govern now our native land.*
>
> *When Minister of our Marine*
> *He lit our coasts with warning lights,*
> *That far upon the sea are seen,*
> *His monuments, on dark dense nights.*
>
> *Peace to the gallant Mitchell's soul,*
> *Remember him, the tried and true.*

John Mercer Johnson

Miramichi's other Father of Confederation was Honourable John Mercer Johnson. Unlike Peter Mitchell who was born here, Johnson was born in Liverpool, England in October 1818. At one year of age, his family came to the Miramichi's Chatham where he grew up, attended grammar school, and later studied law. He was called to the Bar in 1840.

Johnson became a partner in a law firm with Mitchell, but both were interested in politics and eventually pursued that avenue.

Johnson was first elected to the N.B. Legislature in 1850 as a Reformer and entered the Cabinet in 1854. He held successive appointments as Solicitor-General (1854-56), Postmaster General (1857-58), Speaker of the Legislature (1859-62) and Attorney General (1862-65).

Johnson was defeated in 1865, but re-elected again in 1866. With Mitchell he was known as one of the "Smashers" who were for

Confederation. He resigned from the provincial government to run as a Liberal in the new Parliament of Canada, defeating Conservative Thomas F. Gillespie in September 1867.

Prior to that, Johnson had been instrumental in promoting the cause of Confederation. He was a delegate to both the Charlottetown and Quebec conferences, and then to the London conference which finalized the terms of Confederation.

It was reported that Johnson was quite the skater. While in England for the London conference, the Thames froze over, and Johnson dazzled all who watched with his skating ability.

In her "Historical Sketches of Miramichi", Lois Martin records that Johnson also had quite an interest in poetry. Martin says that:

"He had a bent for poetry and one of his religious poems entitled 'Crucifixion Day' is in the possession of one of his great grandsons, Leonard Johnson of Chatham."

Martin also notes that Johnson was quite involved with the Chatham Rifles which he organized and served as "their captain".

After their ten month stay in London, Johnson and Mitchell, were given a complimentary banquet in Chatham upon their return in May, 1867.

In the first election for the Parliament of Canada, Johnson was elected as a Liberal member from Northumberland County, but held that position only fourteen months as he died in Chatham, N.B., November 8, 1868.

Johnson was buried in St. Paul's Churchyard, in Bushville near Chatham Head. There is a monument to his memory, and there was a plaque in the former Chatham post office in his honour.

It is reported that the family saved the ink well and pen that Johnson had used to sign the B.N.A. Act in London as well as the silver and bronze medals presented by Queen Victoria to each of the Fathers of Confederation.

Martin says that Edward J. Russell, great great grandchild of Johnson, has the Bronze Confederation medal presented to Johnson by Queen Victoria, and several volumes of books which also belonged to him.

The lobby wall of the Centennial Building in Fredericton, N.B. has a tribute to Johnson in the form of a quotation dealing with the bringing about of Confederation. It reads:

"From an address delivered in Ottawa November 1, 1864 by the Honourable John Mercer Johnson, Attorney General of New Brunswick and Father of Confederation, born in Liverpool, England 1818."

"...The conference was held when all agreed to set aside their own peculiar opinions for the Common Good, and the advantages of union were so great that all minor differences on political matters should be sunk and forgotten. This is the way that I hope people will meet the question - either declare against it like men, if they believe the union to be without advantage, or if they believe it will prove beneficial, to lay aside all questions of mere party, in order to secure it."

Poet Whalen also had a of tribute to Johnson as he did for Mitchell.

So gifted and so great in many ways
A public man whose record bore no blame
And when our country's history shall be writ
By some sane hand, which doubtless will be done,
This statesman, orator, and brilliant wit
Shall have his own again, his victory won
In that great fight of fifty years ago
That laid the ghost of old abuses low
Bequeathing freedom's gifts from sire to son.

Lord Beaverbrook--Max Aitken

One of the Miramichi's more illustrious sons was Max Aitken, better known as Lord Beaverbrook. Basically a self-made man, Beaverbrook rose to be one of the most influential newspaper men in England and became a multi-millionaire.

Beaverbrook was born in Maple, Ontario in 1879, but moved to the Miramichi when he was ten months old when his father accepted a position as Minister of St. James Presbyterian Church in Newcastle.

The Beaverbrook home in Newcastle.

Beaverbrook received his early education at Harkins Academy in Newcastle where he was described as being only a fair student whose strong point was mathematics. He was anything but a model student. In fact he was described as being mischievous. His favourite authors were Walter Scott and Walter Louis Stevenson.

Beaverbrook did not finish school leaving in grade 10. He was to write later: "If I had the education of my sons to supervise over again, I believe I would not send them to the English Public Schools. I think they would get a better preparation for life at Harkins Academy in Newcastle".

As a boy, Max Aitken spent his time doing odd jobs such as milking cows, picking potato bugs, pumping the organ in his father's church, and carrying firewood. He also had an egg and paper route and produced his own paper called *The Leader* at age 13, a path which he was to follow most of his life.

Beaverbrook's first paper was cut short when his father caught him working into the early morning of the Sabbath, desecrating the holy day.

His egg business has an interesting anecdote. He kept hens, feeding them with household scraps from his home and from neighbours. One day when his eggs fell short of the number required for his orders, he "borrowed" from his mother who was absent at the time.

Shortly after, one his customers asked if the eggs had been fresh. Beaverbrook replied "Why, weren't they?", to which the client replied, "They were the first fresh-laid eggs I have ever seen arrive in the world hard-boiled."Beaverbrook , always quick witted, replied "I was frightened that the thunderstorm we had yesterday would affect the hens".

In his own book "My Early Life" Beaverbrook writes "My own opinion is that the story was cooked and not the egg".

For a while he studied law in Chatham, N.B. under R.B. Bennett. Bennett was credited with asking whether Beaverbrook was working for him, or he for Beaverbrook.

After failing his entrance papers at Dalhousie University in Halifax, N.S., Beaverbrook observed that, "A university career involved unnecessary and useless labour in futile educational pursuits". Instead he decided "Now, I'm going to make money. I'm going to sell what makes money".

Beaverbrook followed his resolve very successfully. He moved to Halifax, N.S. and worked between there and Montreal. He became an important financier, assisting in important bank and steel industries, and the merger of 13 companies. Beaverbrook believed and became living proof of the idea that a man, however small his beginnings and however poor his opportunities, was master of his own fate. By the time he was in his early 20's he had become a millionaire.

Beaverbrook then moved to England where he became involved in both politics and journalism. He was also a great historian, an art lover and was considered a "character" by many who knew him such as Churchill, Stalin, Roosevelt and Bennett.

In tense negotiations at Malta following World War II Beaverbrook was said to have broken the ice as he sang the Miramichi folksong "The Jones Boys". He had Stalin singing it before the night was finished.

In 1910 Max Aitken was elected to the British House of Commons and was knighted in 1911. In 1916 he was made a Baronet and in 1917 raised to Peerage. When he was asked to choose a name for his title, on the advice of his close friend Rudyard Kipling, he took the name "Beaverbrook" after the tiny stream and community in his Miramichi. Kipling told him no one would be able to pronounce "Miramichi".

In 1916 Beaverbrook purchased the *Daily Mail* and commenced to build his newspaper business. He eventually owned a whole network of newspapers which included *The Daily Express, The Times, The Evening Standard* and *The Scottish Daily Express.*

Beaverbrook played important roles in both World Wars. In World War I he served as Minister for Information in the British cabinet and in World War II Winston Churchill appointed him Minister of Air Craft production. This was certainly an important post when one looks at the Battle of Britain. Under Beaverbrook, Spitfire production went round the clock.

In 1942 Beaverbrook served as Minister of Supply, and then from 1943-45 he held the position of Lord Privy Seal, retiring from politics in 1945 to devote his time to his newspaper empire.

Beaverbrook always wanted to be known as a journalist and

that is what he called himself on his passport.

In the latter years of his life Beaverbrook took to writing. He authored a total of 11 books including "My Early Life" in 1964.

A.J.P. Taylor in his biography "Beaverbrook" wrote, "Beaverbrook took as much trouble over his friends as over his staff. He kept a note of all birthdays and also drew his attention to any event in a friend's life. He wanted to be efficient even in his personal kindness".

Taylor adds, "For the most part of his life he gave away more than half of his annual income to charities or to those in distress".

Despite all of his success and world fame, Beaverbrook never forgot his boyhood home on the Miramichi. In 1953 he purchased the "Old Manse" from the church where his father had been minister. The Manse had been his home for the first 18 years of his life. Beaverbrook had it converted to a public library to which he donated 10,000 books.

During the 1950's he was the one who influenced Dr. Louise Manny to begin collecting Miramichi Folksongs, many of which ended up in "The Beaverbrook Collection". He was responsible for providing Louise Manny with the money to restore the Wilson's Point Burial ground now known as the Enclosure. He provided many churches in the Miramichi with organs and chimes.

Beaverbrook gave Newcastle the Beaverbrook Town Hall and Theatre and a skating and hockey rink which was named "The Sinclair Arena" after his friend Edward Sinclair who had loaned him money to go to university. The Sinclair Rink was the victim of a fire and was replaced by the Miramichi Civic Centre which was built on the same site.

Beaverbrook was also given control of the Town Square in the former Newcastle which he restored with a gazebo, including memorials to Peter Mitchell and other pioneers of the Miramichi. There is now a tribute to Louise Manny there as well. Beaverbrook also gave Chatham The Lord Beaverbrook Arena.

Beaverbrook set up university scholarships for promising young students, and gave the University of New Brunswick in

Fredericton a set of chimes for the Lady Beaverbrook Residence and had them programmed to play the tune of "The Jones Boys". In 1947 Beaverbrook was installed as Chancellor of the University of New Brunswick. He also funded the construction of several other buildings and facilities at UNB such as the Aitken Centre. He even visited and spoke to students there. The Beaverbrook Art Gallery and the Beaverbrook Theatre in Fredericton were also his gifts.

All the paintings on the walls of the Senate Chamber in Ottawa, Canada were donated by Lord Beaverbrook.

Beaverbrook was married twice. His first wife was Gladys Drury, the daughter of General Charles Drury. Many years after her death, Beaverbrook married Lady Dunn, the widow of his life long friend Sir James Dunn.

Bust of Beaverbrook in the town square of Newcastle.

Lord Beaverbrook died in London, England in 1964 at the age of 85. However, he rarely missed having an annual visit to his beloved Miramichi. Fittingly, his ashes were returned to the Town Square in Newcastle and placed under a bust carved in his image. "The Beaver" as he was called, finally came home to the river he had always loved.

Miramichi has two streets named after him. They are Aitken Avenue and Beaverbrook Boulevard.

A visit with Tom Donovan:
A Man of Many Visions

MIRAMICHI - Tom Donovan of Red Bank was not your average man. Donovan was a man of many visions. They were visions which he made reality.

Donovan was a retired guidance councillor and teacher, but he was far from idle. Being busy with a special project was nothing new to Donovan. He always did things with a view of the visionary.

Donovan's last project was to follow in the footsteps of Nova Scotia's Pumpkin King, Howard Dill. Although not near Dill's feats by Donovan's own admission, the summer of 1998 was the beginning of some big things. Three pumpkins to be precise.

Donovan bought a package of Dill's seeds and actually called him for advice on how to grow monster pumpkins. In his first attempts, Donovan had reasonable success.

He won first prize at the Miramichi Agricultural Exhibition which takes place the third week of August. His pumpkin weighed over 200 pounds.

For pumpkin growers there are three measurements that are used to approximate the weight of a pumpkin. First they measure the circumference from blossom top to stem in inches. Then they measure ground to ground over the top of the pumpkin on both axis (east/west and north/south) and thirdly, around the middle. They then add the three measurements (in inches) together and multiply by 1.9. On a pumpkin in the 400 pound range, it is accurate to within 20 pounds.

Donovan actually laid a cloth measuring tape under his pumpkins and said that in peak growing times they would grow eight centimetres a day in circumference.

Donovan's second pumpkin went to the Fredericton Exhibition where it won the $100 first prize on September 4 weighing in at 317 pounds with the next closest being 60 pounds less. Donovan figured that had he not picked it when he did, it would have reached about 500 pounds.

"Although I won first prize, I suspect that many would not have cut their pumpkins as early as I did, and there probably would be many as large around," said Donovan.

Trying to grow large pumpkins is no easy task.

"We had heavy rains early in the summer and you have to shield the pumpkins from weather like that. I built a 100 foot wind shield to protect mine from prevailing winds," said Donovan.

"The leaves are so big, that a wind will actually turn the plant over," said Donovan.

You have to allow a minimum of 30 feet between each large pumpkin to get maximum growth. A vine shouldn't go beyond 10 to 12 feet either side of the actual pumpkin. Donovan said that this being his first year, he made the mistake of having two pumpkins only seven feet apart and that probably prevented them from growing larger.

Donovan also added that you have to hand pollinate the blossom for optimum results. He explained how the female blossom has a small pumpkin about the size of a large marble or plumper at the base of the blossom, while the male does not have any.

"There are ten spots that must be touched with the male pollen. A bee might only get five or six. The pumpkin would still grow, but not to its greatest size."

Donovan would pick off 100 to 150 blossoms each day so other pumpkins would not start and thereby take nutrients from the main pumpkin. He said that the male blossoms grow closer to the pumpkin while the female blossoms are further out.

"The plant seems to sense that the blossoms are being picked and it produces more to compensate. Nature is a wonderful thing," said Donovan.

"Some of my friends would make fun of me when I was hand pollinating my plants. You can imagine what they were saying about me being kinky with my pumpkins," he laughed.

You have to feed the plants a pound of soluble fertilizer high in phosphorous every five days until they get large, and then you balance it about 20/20. He used a weeping hose to give his pumpkins steady moisture because they needed a lot of water.

In the peak growing season you have to be careful because the pumpkin can grow so fast that it will literally explode and all you will have left is a blob.

Donovan had a few problems in the early part of the season. First he had to treat the plants chemically to get them going, and then he had trouble with the cucumber beetle. To make matters worse, he had to battle a harsh growing climate.

"The Annapolis Valley is a zone six which is the warmest in Atlantic Canada. It is not surprising that they grow the largest there. They can get up to 25 1/2 pounds a day in the peak of the season, and they have a lot more peak days that we do here. There were two pumpkins over 1,000 pounds at the Windsor, N.S. competitions last year," said Donovan.

"But here in Red Bank we are in a zone 3. Napan for example is just below the former Chatham and it is zone 4. Heath Steele Mines northwest of us, is in zone 2. We cut across agricultural zones rather quickly here. Normally in the rest of the country you might go 200 miles before changing a zone."

"Howard Dill gets 125 days from seed to full life. We might get half that here. When the temperature hits 52 degrees Fahrenheit pumpkins will stop growing. The metabolism shuts down, and it is a really hard job to get it going again. Sometimes we can get those temperatures in late July and mid August," said Donovan.

Donovan got into growing giant pumpkins strictly "for fun".

"I did it for the fun of it. It is nice to see the amazement on people's faces when they see an extremely large pumpkin. There was one young kid that was actually scared to go near it to get his picture taken."

There was also the imp in Donovan.

"I get a lot of school children and classes coming as a group to visit the orchard and to see the pumpkins. I have buried a wire under the pumpkin and have a tape recorder with a 20 second delay on it. I'll step in the barn and turn it on and then take the kids to the pumpkin patch."

"When the kids get close, the tape inside the pumpkin comes on and says `Don't sit on me. How would you feel if someone sat on you?', Then it says, `Don't just stand there. Say Hello Mr. Pumpkin', and the kids then usually do what it says," recalled Donovan with a chuckle.

Tom Donovan with one of his "monster" pumpkins.

But growing pumpkins was only Donovan's latest vision. Donovan's interest in children is observed in the facilities he created for them. His yard had a huge two seat wooden airplane as large as you might see in a circus ride, chained between two trees on the hillside. Many a kid has taken a special ride into the imaginary blue on Donovan's plane.

And if they did not wish to fly in the plane, they could take a run holding the rope Donovan had tied to a big tree and sail off over the hillside some 30 feet in the air.

"When a group of kids were here last week they couldn't get the hang of taking a run with the rope and then jumping off the hill, so I gave them a demonstration. When I swung back one little kid said "You are one cool old man." I didn't know if he was insulting me or complimenting me," said Donovan with a laugh.

Over the years he has had many interesting projects which have fascinated his own kids and have provided entertainment for much of the community.

He built and operated a lighted outdoor rink where the community played hockey and skated for 14 years. He built a 500 foot toboggan slide that went down his side hill and he would flood it every few days. It was not the faint of heart that dared take the trip down as you could reach speeds of 40 to 50 m.p.h..

Donovan also had an apple orchard of close to 600 trees although harsh winters and too friendly deer and bear have dwindled the number to 300.

"Most of my friends drive miles and miles to hunt deer, and I can't get rid of them, and I don't hunt myself," said Donovan who has also had visits from bear, moose, porcupine and coyote.

Yet he still sold his apples, and treated every class of school kids to an apple when they arrived, taking the time to show them the proper way to turn the apple and then snap it from the tree.

Donovan also had a huge garden with literally over an acre of corn which provided many a feast for the local bear population. Every night Donovan would drive his car back to the orchard so the car lights would scare the deer and bears from his trees.

He allowed local bee keepers to place their hives on his property to facilitate the pollination of his trees, and naturally the bears would round out their diet with the honey, destroying the hives in the process.

The idea of always having fresh carrots through the winter was one that Donovan relished. He did this by covering them with a mulch and plastic. In the middle of winter he would simply brush away the snow and dig them as needed. Donovan also had a large number of strawberry and raspberry plants but unfortunately their fruits were limited to the summer season.

The Donovan's unusual home is a huge barn-shaped three story structure with a 21 foot high cathedral ceiling and fireplace in the living room. It was Donovan's project from start to finish. Before it was completed Donovan had actually cleared 12 to 14 acres of forest for his home and surroundings, drawn the blueprints for his house, cut his own lumber, had the logs sawed, and then planed them himself before actually building the house.

A horseshoe shaped driveway overlooks the Northwest Miramichi a few miles below Red Bank. It has several decks offering a very scenic view. Donovan retrieved the huge chains that were used in the Northwest Booms to hold logs and painted them black. They are strewn between the cedar logs which fence the upper part of his drive-around.

Adjacent to the house is his barn. But it is not your usual barn, or is it used for the usual purpose. It is more of a community center and a small museum. It has the stained glass windows from the former church in Blackville and the pew benches around the inside. There Donovan held his annual barn dances giving any monies taken at the door to different charities.

The inside of the barn is especially unique. One end has a huge mural painted by Glen Hall, an art teacher at North and South Esk Regional High School, and his students. Donovan explained that the river actually curves the way it is painted.

"It is based on the forestry maps. People don't realize that there is that much of a curve in the river here, but there is."

Inserted throughout the mural are pictures of various smaller scenes such as the old church and the first steamboat to come up the river as well as a number of other vignettes from the area as it was 100 years ago.

The opposite wall has a huge 10 by 45 foot floor to ceiling map depicting the whole Miramichi River system. All communities and islands are marked. On this map are maybe 200 photos of early lumbering activities complete with accurate dates and information.

During his last summer Donovan built a greenhouse in front of his home on the side hill. A beautiful perennial garden extends 160 by 15 feet around the greenhouse. This provided a gorgeous backdrop for his daughter's wedding festivities.

"I don't sell anything from it, but a lot of the older people will drop in for some peppers or late cucumbers", said Donovan. He also had several walnut trees which produce quality nuts.

Donovan also planted about 75 different rose bushes around the driveway in front of his house, and each one has a specially carved wooden sign telling the kind of bush it is.

His interest in identifying his plants led him to invite botanist Norman Stewart to come over for a day to name many of the plants around his property. Both the English and Latin names are written on cedar plaques which he had planned to erect along his walking trail.

Donovan also built a 1 1/4 mile road suitable for a car leading to the back of his property. As I was about to leave, Donovan said that I had to drive with him back to his woodlot where he had created a covered bridge and picnic area beside a huge spring. The spring actually becomes a brook that flows the length of his 100 acres. This tireless man was also working on a hiking trail along the brook.

We drove by the spot to the turning area which has a sculptured sign "White Birch Lane".

"Isn't it a pretty sight with all the birch trees? I decided to name it White Birch Lane," said Donovan.

We returned to the picnic area some 40 feet off to the side of the road. It boasts a huge spring about eight feet across coming out of the base of a tree that is home to a garter snake.

As we walked along Donovan said:

"I wonder if the garter snake is there? There is one that actually lives in the spring. He is there every time I come. I must ask Harry Walker (local nature lover) about it," said Donovan. And sure enough the snake is there curled up in the water.

Donovan has made a little cedar trough with water flowing out of it as the spring begins its journey under a red cedar covered bridge just wide enough to walk through and about 25 feet long.

Donovan has given it an antique touch with signs from olden days. One end reads "No Faster Than A Walk" and the other "Walk Your Horse Across Or Pay The Fine".

"I tried to make it more real by putting up the old signs," he explained.

On one side of the bridge is another sign which reads "O'Donnabain Rosa Bridge". He took that sign's inscription from an actual bridge in Ireland.

There is another little spring coming in just beside the main one. Donovan built another bridge over it. It is bowed, and so he appropriately gave it the name "Rainbow Bridge" with a sign painted accordingly.

There is also a picnic table with a top covering it to keep out the rain and a barbeque behind it.

All structures are made of cedar which Donovan has cut himself from his property, and then shaped out with his powersaw. Even the walking planks to the bridge have been individually cut with his powersaw.

Donovan's amazing abilities extended beyond his own property. He was known as a big community supporter. He was one of the prime forces in building the Rink and Recreation Center in Renous, on the committee which raised money for the Miramichi Valley High School pool, and one of the members responsible for establishing the Community College on the Miramichi.

As I finished my visit, I was told to pick some apples to take home, but not to pick off the two flagged trees as there are two classes coming that week and he wanted to make sure that each of the children actually had the experience of picking an apple themselves.

I got into my car and drove home wondering what Donovan's next visionary project would be. Little did I know that his projects would come to a sudden end.

Tom Donovan died unexpectedly January 29, 1999, while playing hockey in the Renous Arena which he helped build. The people of Miramichi will miss him.

A Day With Edmond Robichaud
"Outdoorsman and Trapper"

Mr. Morris Green, a teacher, former New Brunswick Liberal Cabinet Minister and the son-in-law of Edmond Robichaud, fondly recalls a day spent with this well known outdoorsman and trapper. The following is an account in Green's own words of a memorable day with Edmond Robichaud.

August 4, 1993 my wife Peggy dropped me off at Ace Leasing in Newcastle to pick up the "S-10" GMC for the journey to the woods, and a journey back in time through the memory of Edmond Robichaud.

After buying a few more necessities from Sobey's, I arrived at 377 Jane St. where Edmond waited. With his minimal pack, fishing rod and jug of good water and my elaborate supplies, we set out.

Steve Allen's was our first stop where Edmond obtained a trout license. Leo Babineau sat in a chair and questioned Edmond about his destination. After a bit of banter we travelled north to the Fraser-Burchill Road.

Along the way I was told how the country had changed. "Tote" roads were the only means of travel in the early thirties when Edmond travelled and worked in the area.

Gilbert Pattles was also a favourite topic of conversation. It was with him that Edmond had spent four or five years trapping in this area and on through to Bathurst.

Edmond recalled with pleasure a visit he had made to Bathurst with Gilbert. Gilbert's dad was very pleased to see them and provided them with a grub stake for the winter's trapping.

Gilbert's mother from Eel Ground had made sure that Gilbert had learned all the ways of the natives, including how to survive in the woods. Edmond learned the same lessons from Gilbert when they were partners.

Gilbert had a great respect and love for his mother. One indication of his devotion was his making of prayer sticks which were carved in tree shape, from one stick like we would make to start a fire. Once made, these sticks became the symbolic centre of a ceremony which called upon the spirits of the departed for help and guidance.

Other parts of his religion included praying to the spirits that inhabited all things, both living and non-living. Gilbert believed that he was only part of a creation that had all other things as equals. His role was to be the best he could within this greater world without unnecessarily harming other things. The mother of all was the earth. It was the source of all existence. Reverence and respect for all underlay all of Gilbert's actions.

Another thing that Gilbert learned from his mother were his legal rights as a native. Edmond said that Gilbert always carried his treaty wrapped in deer skin. He sometimes had to produce it to force white men to allow him to hunt and trap in his traditional ways.

Gilbert's family were very kind to Edmond and he spent much time at their home in Eel Ground. Gilbert's wife operated a grocery store in the village. She would always give her husband money for necessities.

Another day, Edmond told me how he and Gilbert had met. Edmond had been hired to work as a cookie at a lumber camp. As the portage wagon on which he was a passenger stopped to rest the horses, two men approached and asked Edmond for some food.

Edmond explained that he was only working there, but he would ask the teamster. The teamster simply said that he had to go down the trail for a walk. In his absence, Edmond filled a large oat sack with bacon, bread, potatoes, and anything else he could find from the winter's food supply. Gilbert and his companion simply took the food and left.

Sometime later in the fall, Gilbert appeared at the camp and gave Edmond some fox skins in appreciation. This was the beginning of a lifelong friendship.

Later, Gilbert asked Edmond to become his trapping partner. They had quite a career together. I think Edmond thought of Gilbert as a second father. He was the man who showed him how to live in and with the wilderness at a time when the word still meant something in New Brunswick.

Edmond told me that when they travelled in the woods, they only needed some salt, pepper, a prepared flour mix for bannock and powdered milk. All the rest was provided by nature.

Among the foods eaten were beaver, cat tails, inner bark of spruce, berries, leaves of some plants, fish, deer, moose and partridge. The tail of the beaver was put in the fire to cook. After, it was taken out and cut open. The meat had the consistency of jelly and was very rich in protein. Apparently, one could only eat small portions at a time.

The hindquarters of a beaver were also cooked and the meat was very tasty. The beaver's dried castor was used as a great cure for the common cold. Edmond still had some that is over 40 years old, a testament to his good health.

All parts of the cat tail can be eaten. The mature head can be ground into flour for bread, the young stem can be boiled and eaten, and the roots dried and saved as another cure for the cold.

The inner bark of the spruce was important as a source of vitamins to prevent scurvy. Alder bark could be used for the same thing. I also learned that the roots of the alder were the ropes used by the natives for all purposes. These long, strong, flexible fibers were always at hand. Some of their uses were to tie the top of a wigwam together, make nets to catch fish, or just to tie things together so the women could carry them more easily.

Edmond told me of one native who had three women. One was big strong and rugged. Her job was to carry supplies, game or anything else that had to be done. The second was to make and fill snowshoes, make clothes, moccasins or manufacture any other requirements as well as to cook. The third was young and pretty. Her role was to be the sleeping companion to the man. It was quite a complete family and apparently worked very well.

When we were eating our lunch at Sheephouse Brook, Edmond mentioned how surprised Father Murdock was to discover how Gilbert and Edmond washed dishes and clothes.

Both were placed in separate nets made from onion bags. The dishes had white sand added. The bag was then placed in a white water current and left. The same was done with the clothes. Instead of sand, soap was added. The result was clean dishes and clean clothes for the two inventive men. Edmond called these their automatic dish and clothes washers.

The journey to Sheephouse Brook was nostalgic as Edmond kept saying how he could imagine the stone age natives travelling stealthily through the woods in search of game 10,000 years ago. The many types of trees, rugged rocks and crags, the unusual quietness, the stream, and Edmond's imagination took us both back to that time of long ago.

Edmond started talking about the cave he had seen when we had first visited the site some two years before. I didn't remember the cave as such, but wasn't about to argue. When it comes to observing nature, I have learned to let Edmond be my guide.

The view of Sheephouse Falls was spectacular. As we walked along, Edmond picked up a piece of flint. He showed me how this extremely hard rock could be flaked off to manufacture arrowheads, spearheads, and many other tools for the stone age people who had lived there. The vicinity of the falls was a treasure trove for this activity.

We travelled along further to Lambs' Falls, where we found a cave. After saying that he thought it was man made, Edmond then conjured up a picture of a stone age man sitting in the cave waiting for game, cooking dinner, or perhaps hiding from threatening animals.

Just to satisfy my cynical mind, I decided to take a look before we left. The cave, which was now just an overhang, was cool and welcoming on this very hot day. Sitting there, I began to feel Edmond's conviction.

Looking around behind me, I found, on a stone shelf, a piece of flint with a square hole punched in one end. It looked like part of a spear head or perhaps an amulet worn by some stone age man or woman. Regardless of what it was, this rock proved again to me that this man knew what he was talking about.

What a treat it was to have had the privilege to share this day with someone who had not only lived a full and varied life, but who had also thought deeply about it.

On the way home, Edmond told me about living with Father Murdock on the Bartibogue about eight miles from the Big Arch. He told me about the eight and three quarter pound trout caught by young Vince Keoghan who also lived with Father Murdock.

Apparently, the young man didn't catch it according to the rules, and to hide his misdeed from the strict priest, he inserted a hook in the fish's mouth. Regardless, it was quite a meal for these wilderness people.

One time Edmond became very sick with dysentery. Father Murdock could do nothing to help him. After about three days, Gilbert

Pattles arrived and saw his friend sick. After the priest had expressed his inability to cure the illness, Gilbert, said he knew how.

He gathered pith from the pockets on balsam trees and mixed it with hot water and sugar. A dose of this remedy at noon and evening had Edmond up and around the next day.

As we neared home, it was clear that there was still much Edmond could teach us all not only about the woods, but about life as well. Perhaps it was his primitive experience combined with his intelligence and sensitivity that made him so wise. Although he thought I had done him a favour by taking him out for the day, it was I who had gained.

Stanford George McKibbon
(November 8, 1891 - August 4, 1974)

The Miramichi culture has been created by the land, its resources and its people. Stanford McKibbon was one of the many people who contributed to the development of the Miramichi culture and the flavour of the region. His story is best told by the members of his own family.

Stanford G. McKibbon was born in 1891 in the settlement of Exmoor, Northumberland County, New Brunswick, the son of John J. McKibbon and Evis (Mullin) McKibbon. He lived near Wildcat Brook and attended school at the Exmoor School house. In his early years he operated a small local store which he eventually sold to his brother Edmond. At the age of twenty-eight, Stanford attended Business College in Fredericton. After finishing his course he was employed in Newcastle as manager of the Creamery, owned by William Sullivan.

On October 10, 1923, Stanford married Emeline Mary Bryenton and they travelled to New York City by train for their honeymoon. The McKibbons established their new home and business on a

99 year lease on the Indian Reserve in the village of Red Bank. They built a large general store, including a warehouse, a barn, and a garage. For fifty years they worked together in the store and raised a family of nine children; seven daughters, Barbara, Elsie, Norma, Louise, Faye, Ruth, and Arlene, and two sons, Guy and Edward (Ned).

All of these children were born at their home in Red Bank. Local residents were employed at the store and also in the house where two maids worked long busy days. Stanford also established a lumbering business which at times provided significant levels of employment for men from the local area and beyond and ran a bus line from Red Bank to Newcastle. (For more on the bus line see the chapter on "The Red Bank Cannon Ball".)

One of Stanford George McKibbon's many business ventures that supported and employed many Miramichiers.

Stanford did not entirely accept the notion of daylight savings time. To avoid confusion he set his own time and his bus schedule to coincide with the train schedule which remained all year on Atlantic Standard Time. This was fine for railway pickups and deliveries, but tended to cause some confusion for other residents who for the most part went on "fast" time for the summer months.

Stanford was very old fashioned in many ways, but he was also very clever and innovative. In the early 1930's, he built a snowmobile powered by a Ford automobile engine. He equipped it with double rubber tracks with skis handmade from birch which he bent into shape using steam over a tub of boiling water. The first time he tried it he confidently drove up the high hill behind his house with his little daughter Barbara on the seat beside him. The main purpose of the snowmobile was to provide reliable transport to haul supplies from Newcastle during the stormy winter months. The snowmobile travelled the river road (on the ice) and was so successful that Stanford later built a second similar machine.

For two years, Stanford even took on the responsibility of plowing the road between Red Bank and Newcastle using his own truck plow in order for his bus service to continue as much as possible during those winter months. This proved to be of great benefit to the community and the practice was soon taken over more consistently by the government.

Christmas was a wonderful time for all of the family. Everyone was kept extra busy with customers in the store. All of the family would participate in the joy of wrapping the many presents to be given to friends and relatives. Stanford and Emeline would send more than one hundred gift boxes to elderly or sick people with juices, fruits, chocolates, ginger ale, and in some boxes even a small bottle of brandy would be slipped in for "medicinal" purposes. When Stanford took his own daily "medicine", he would usually include his traditional toast, "Here goes happy days".

On Christmas night and on other special occasions throughout the year, many relatives and friends would gather at the McKibbon home. These times together were particularly enjoyable and memorable because of the lively music. Emeline played the piano, her brother Murdock played the mouth organ and a cousin, Norman Mather played the violin. They would all sing, dance, tell stories, and enjoy a great variety of good food.

Stanford was a great family man. He and Emeline always had high regard and devotion for each other. None of the family can ever remember their parents arguing or saying anything disagreeable to each other. On Sunday afternoons all the family including one or more of the neighbour children would crowd into their 1936 Ford to be taken for a long and pleasant drive. Emeline packed a nice picnic lunch which they would enjoy on blankets spread out in a sunny field along the way. The McKibbon-Bryenton family began a tradition of having large extended family picnics nearly every summer. That tradition has continued to the present time.

Out of concern for his children's safety, Stanford never allowed them to own or ride a bicycle. They found this quite strange particularly when they learned many years later that as a young man Stanford had actually owned and driven a motorcycle. In 1912, at the age of 20, he worked on the construction of the new Morrissy Bridge in Newcastle. He stayed at the Royal Hotel and proudly motored about on his own Harley-Davidson.

Stanford had a constant fear of fire. Many homes and businesses had been destroyed by the Red Bank fire of June 1923. Every summer his family had to fight fires which were started on the blueberry plains behind their house. Stanford kept large barrels of rainwater all along the back of his house and he would not allow grass to be planted, but instead kept sand all around his buildings.

Always an entrepreneur, Stanford began a business when he recognized a need. In the 1940's he opened an ice cream parlour and in the early 1960's Stanford opened a restaurant. By this time some of his children were fully involved in his enterprises and one of his daughters, Norma, operated and managed the restaurant business.

After World War II Stanford purchased four army trucks. He sold one and converted three into lumber trucks. He recognized that in adverse conditions they would outperform other trucks as they were each equipped with four wheel drive and a heavy duty winch. Following the war he was able also to buy sections of old airplanes which he dismantled for the valuable parts. The huge airplane wheels were used to build large trailers for the army trucks. Hauling pulp and firewood was made more efficient with the rugged trucks and larger loads were made possible by the trailers.

Loading pulp onto his trucks was always a slow difficult job. In order to make this job easier, Stanford designed a log loader which was then built by his son Guy. The machine was run by cables and designed so that the boom could be adjusted to permit ease of use anywhere. This was particularly useful as the boom could be levelled to swing horizontally even if the loader was parked on a hill.

Cutting, splitting, and stacking firewood was always a big job. One summer Stanford cut thirty-three truck loads of firewood. During the winter months Stanford operated twelve wood stoves. There were three in the house, two in the store, two in the restaurant, one in each garage, and three on the buses.

Stanford's store made a significant contribution to the local community. The store was well stocked with a great variety of merchandise including all kinds of food, as well as dishes, toys, hardware, window glass, paint, bucksaws, axes, peaveys, boots, shoes, clothing, and fishing gear. Most of the groceries were available only in bulk. Puncheons of molasses, bags or barrels of white sugar, brown sugar, flour, white beans, oatmeal, barley, cornmeal, tea, dates, prunes, dried apples, fig cookies and nuts all had to be weighed and were sold by the pound. The animal feed was kept in a warehouse near the store in Red Bank.

Occasionally a shipment of dresses would arrive from Montreal. The seven daughters would find this an exciting event and would promptly pick out their favourites. The real customers happily made do very nicely with what was left.

A day at the store began precisely at 7:00 a.m. just as the bell rang in the local church. Katie Bryenton's first job of the morning was to pump up 10 gallons of gasoline to be ready for the first customer.

The McKibbon store provided supplies for many logging and sporting camps. The four wheel drive army trucks travelled over almost impassable woods roads to deliver to these operations. In making deliveries to the Forks of the Little Southwest Miramichi River, it was necessary to ford the river as the camps were located on the opposite bank, taking advantage of the best view down the river.

Sometimes when Stanford was making winter deliveries, local boys would run out and grab onto the rear bumper of the car and slide along behind on the slippery road. On one occasion a lad by the name of Valmore Stewart readied himself behind the car just as Stanford, unaware of his presence, backed up. When Valmore appeared from under the front of the car, Stanford got a glimpse of him as he fled the scene. For several days after Stanford inquired about the well being of the boys in that area. Of course Val said nothing at all.

Stanford had a large ice house on his property which not only provided ice for his store freezers but also for sale to his customers. The ice was sold for $1 a cake, no matter what size! The store's walk-in freezers were kept cold with ice that was chopped finely and put daily inside a double wall from overhead.

Men were hired in the winter to cut the ice in the river and haul it by horses and sled to the ice house where it was covered with sawdust. Stanford recognized the need for quicker and easier access to the river ice and so he devised a gasoline powered ice saw. He used a 6 cylinder Chev motor mounted on a large sled frame to drive an incredible 6 foot diameter blade. As this contraption was hauled by an army truck over the frozen river, ice chips would fly high into the air.

After electricity was installed and the ice house was no longer required, Stanford and Ned removed the old saw dust and ice. As they got down to the last of the ice, Stanford recovered an old axe which he had left in the ice over forty years earlier.

On one occasion during an attempt to use an army truck for hauling the ice, one of the employees accidentally drove the truck through the ice hole into the river. Then at low tide, Stanford and his young son Ned endured the icy water to secure large logs alongside and under the truck in an attempt to raise it. After three changes of tides the truck was finally recovered.

One spring day in 1954, Guy and Ned were driving one of the buses down the Little Southwest Road. They spotted a fire from a distance and they thought it might be their own home or store. Just then the steering mechanism on the bus broke. Subsequently they lost control of the bus and it upset at the Oxbow. The boys hitched a ride and arrived at Red Bank to witness a great calamity, as the old Red Bank covered bridge burned and fell into the river (April 13, 1954). This old bridge had the proud distinction of being the second longest covered bridge in the world.

The McKibbons were especially kind-hearted to elderly people and often invited them as guests into their home for extended periods of time. Being with the large family was most pleasant for these otherwise lonely people. Stanford had a great concern that the elderly should not be placed in the "poor house" as he called the government sponsored residences in those days.

Stanford's thoughtfulness and consideration was appreciated by many. Once when he went to Saint John on a business trip, he stopped by the convent to visit a young Miramichi nun. When the Mother Superior announced to Sister Mary Murphy that there was "a gentleman to see you," Sister knew immediately it would be Stanford McKibbon. She later related, "Who else would take the time to go to a convent to see a homesick girl?"

In the 1960's, the Lyttleton Pentecostal church under the leadership of Rev. Herman Trenholm asked to hold Saturday evening drive-in church services on the veranda of Stanford's home. Although the McKibbons went to a different church, for years many people came and sat in their cars to enjoy the lively gospel music and preaching.

During the period that the McKibbons operated their store, times were difficult for many of the people in Red Bank and the surrounding communities. Stanford was a businessman and did not hesitate to use a barter system with local farmers. Bartered goods included beef, pork, chicken, eggs, milk, vegetables and fruit. Customers often bought their food and supplies on credit and, not surprisingly, some were often unable to pay their bills.

Once when Stanford returned from an attempt to collect some of that which was owed, Emeline inquired about his success. He told her he didn't receive any money, but he loaned a man five dollars.

Stanford's store provided the necessary service of making deliveries to his many rural customers. Orders would come in by telephone and boxes would be prepared for the next delivery run. Stanford's daughter Ruth, even as a young teenager, would make deliveries using a touring car which had the back seat removed to make room for grocery boxes.

On one particular occasion, Emeline and her daughter Arlene were driving along and stopped to pick up an elderly man who was walking along the road. As expected, he promptly jumped into the back seat. Emeline noticed that he seemed to sit up unusually close to the front seat, even grabbing on to the back of the front seat itself. After he got out both Arlene and Emeline were greatly amused when at the same time they realized that they weren't driving the family car at all. They were in the delivery car, and that poor old man in the back hadn't even a seat to sit on!

On another occasion Ned hurriedly jotted down a telephone order for groceries. Norma promptly filled the order and sent it with Ned on the next delivery up the Little Southwest. On his way back, Ned was waved down by an elderly lady on the side of the road. She complained that she had been given the wrong delivery. Her box contained a bottle of vanilla, a bag of icing sugar, and a pint of cream. She excitedly exclaimed that there must be some mistake as her order simply called for Vanilla Ice Cream!

Stanford was very observant of and appreciative of nature. He and Emeline looked forward to their many outings to their little camp on the beautiful Peabody Lake where they enjoyed excellent trout fishing. In anticipation of each trip, they packed their car with enough supplies to last for several days and in the early years they even loaded a large rubber boat onto the roof. The rubber boat was later replaced with an aluminum one.

On one occasion while crossing the river with Jimmy (Hurley) Kingston, Stanford observed what he called a sleeping fish in the water. When he related the story of the "sleeping" fish, people didn't believe him. Years later, much to the delight of his family, a Jacques Cousteau television program referred to the proven reality of sleeping fish.

Stanford was also well-known in the community as a story-teller. His stories were often very humourous and were always told in great detail.

For his time period he was also quite well travelled. On more than one occasion he went by boat from Saint John to the famous Boston Sportsmen's Show. In 1939, he and Emeline attended the Worlds Fair in New York where he used his hand compass to travel around the huge fair grounds. This 1939 fair was most impressive to him and he talked about it for many years.

During his visit there he purchased asbestos fireproof doors which he had shipped home to be used in the construction of a walk-in vault for his store. Stanford and Emeline returned to New York twenty-five years later for the 1964 Worlds Fair.

Stanford's oldest son Guy was an excellent mechanic, no doubt a result of his early exposure to so much machinery. Guy continued to keep his father's vehicles and equipment in working order until his untimely death in 1964. The loss of their eldest son had a profound effect on both Emeline and Stanford. Their grief continued for many years.

In the early 1970's, Stanford's garage and attached warehouse were destroyed by fire. A year or so later the barn burned down during the night and by the fall of 1972, his large general store also burned to the ground.

As Stanford got older, he solicited the help of his daughter Ruth to help him to make a tombstone for himself and for Emeline. Under Stanford's instruction, Ruth cast a large monument out of cement. She also did the tedious work required for the inscription. The marker now stands in St. Stephen's United Church Cemetery at Red Bank.

In the summer of 1974, the Red Bank Indian Reserve revoked Stanford's 99 year land occupation lease forcing the elderly McKibbons to relocate. They moved to an old house in Sunny Corner which required extensive renovations. The move was quite traumatic and upsetting for Stanford. In early August of that same summer he died leaving his wife, one son, and seven daughters.

Later that year his old house in Red Bank was burned to the ground. All that remained was the old cement vault at the rear of the store.

Above all, Stanford was a man who loved honesty. This is proven by a story of a day when he was in Saint John, N.B.. A man on the street came up to Stanford and asked him for fifty cents to buy a bottle of beer. Stanford was so impressed that the man did not lie about the intention of his request that he gave him the money.

A short time later, Stanford entered the liquor store. In the front of the line was the man to whom he had given the money. When the man saw Stanford, he said, "Sir, you come and take my place, and I'll take yours".

Information compiled April 1999:
Ruth (McKibbon) Silliker
Edward (Ned) McKibbon
Barbara (McKibbon) Bruce

About the Author

Doug Underhill was born in Newcastle and has lived on the Miramichi all of his life. He graduated from Harkins High School before attending St. Thomas University in Fredericton. He obtained his B.A. in 1968 and B. Ed. in 1969.

He has taught English at Harkins High School and Miramichi Valley High School where he is currently English Department Head.

He has six previous books to his credit. They include three children's books: *The Popcorn Cat and Pumpkin Moon*, *The Popcorn Cat and Pumpkin Moon Make New Friends* and *Popcorn and Pumpkin Save Tommy's Christmas*; two books of poetry, *The Lazy Time of Day* and *Only The Salt* and a humourous *Miramichi Dictionary*.

Doug Underhill is also a sports journalist and freelance writer for Moncton's *The Times & Transcript*, Miramichi's *The Miramichi Leader/Weekend* and Fredericton's *The Gleaner*. An avid outdoorsman, he also writes a weekly fishing column for these papers.

Doug has given numerous reading and workshops on writing in New Brunswick schools, and has read on CBC Radio. With Bob Gillis he produced three videos titled *The Dungarvon Whooper*, *The Headless Nun* and *The Great Miramichi Fire of 1825*.

A founding member of the Writers Federation of New Brunswick, Doug has served as one of its directors for many years. In addition he has represented New Brunswick on the Atlantic Canada National Book Festival Committee.

About the Illustrator

Karen Wheaton grew up in the Miramichi and graduated from North and South Esk Regional High. She did the illustrations for *The Popcorn Cat and Pumpkin Moon*, *The Popcorn Cat and Pumpkin Moon Make New Friends* and *Popcorn and Pumpkin Save Tommy's Christmas*. She is a talented artist and musician who presently operates her own studio "Cornflower Design" where she specializes in floral arrangements and decorative painting.